CONFIRMATION AND THE CHARISMATA

Theodore R. Jungkuntz

Wipf & Stock
PUBLISHERS
Eugene, Oregon

Wipf and Stock Publishers
199 W 8th Ave, Suite 3
Eugene, OR 97401

Confirmation and the Charismata
By Jungkuntz, Theodore R.
Copyright©1997 by Jungkuntz, Theodore R.
ISBN: 1-57910-044-9
Publication date 6/23/1997
Previously published by University Press of America, 1997

To my parents,

Otto and Clara (dec.) Jungkuntz,

without whose spiritual nurture
this book would not be what it is.

Acknowledgements

I am grateful for permission from the designated
publishers to cite at some length from previously published works as follows: pages 8-11, frequent cita-
tions from the Revised Standard Version of the Bible,
copyrighted 1946, 1952 © 1971, 1973 (Division of
Christian Education of the National Council of Churches
of Christ in the USA); pages 57-60, a greatly condensed
citation from Martin Chemnitz, Examination of the Council of Trent, Part II, translated by Fred Kramer (Concordia Publishing House, St. Louis, Mo.); pp.90-91,
an extended quotation from Martin Luther, "On the Councils and the Church", in Luther's Works, American Edition, Vol. 41 (Fortress Press, Philadelphia, Pa.).

TABLE OF CONTENTS

Page

ACKNOWLEDGEMENTS v

TABLE OF CONTENTS vii

INTRODUCTION: THE PROBLEM - THE WHENCE
              AND THE WHITHER OF CONFIRMATION. . 1

CHAPTER ONE: CONFIRMATION IN THE NEW TESTAMENT. 3

    I.   Jesus' Confirmation. 3

    II. The Apostles' Confirmation 5

    III. The Believers' Confirmation 7

    IV. Summary: The Whence and the Whither of
         Confirmation in the New Testament. . . . 15

         Footnotes. 16

CHAPTER TWO: CONFIRMATION IN THE FIRST FIVE
              CENTURIES. 19

    I.   Confirmation-Chrismation in the Apostol-
         ic Church. 20

    II. Confirmation-Chrismation in the Pre-
         Nicene Church. 22

    III. Confirmation-Chrismation in the Post-
         Nicene Church. 25

         Footnotes. 27

CHAPTER THREE: CONFIRMATION IN THE MEDIEVAL
                CHURCH (500-1500). 29

    I.   Confirmation in the Early Middle Ages. . 29

    II. Confirmation in the High Middle Ages . . 33

    III. Confirmation Revitalization Attempts in
         the Late Middle Ages 36

    IV. Summary: The Whence and the Whither of
         Confirmation in the Medieval Church. . . 39

                                                          Page

            Footnotes   40

CHAPTER FOUR :   CONFIRMATION IN THE SIXTEENTH
                CENTURY REFORMATION.   43

    I. Confirmation for Luther and his fol-
        lowers.   44

   II. Confirmation in Lutheran Confessional
        Theology.   50

  III. Confirmation in the Reformed and Ana-
        baptist Traditions.   52

   IV. Confirmation in Roman Catholic Refor-
        mation Theology   55

        Footnotes   60

CHAPTER FIVE :   CONFIRMATION - POST-REFORMATION
                UP TO THE PRESENT ERA.   65

    I. Confirmation after Ignatius of Loyola . .   66

   II. Confirmation after English Puritanism . .   67

  III. Confirmation after German Pietism   69

   IV. Confirmation after Rationalism and
        Revivalism.   72

    V. Confirmation after Renewal Attempts in
        the Nineteenth Century.   75

        Footnotes   77

CHAPTER SIX :   CONFIRMATION IN THE TWENTIETH CEN-
                TURY - THE CHANGING SHAPE OF THE
                QUESTION.   81

    I. Confirmation and the Liturgical Renewal .   82

   II. Confirmation and the Pedagogical Renewal.   86

  III. Confirmation and the Charismatic Renewal.   89

   IV. Discussion Theses Regarding Confirmation
        and the Charismata.   97

Page

Footnotes 100

BIBLIOGRAPHY. 107

ABOUT THE AUTHOR. 115

x

THE PROBLEM:

THE WHENCE AND THE WHITHER OF CONFIRMATION

In a text very suggestive of Christian baptism we hear Jesus saying:

> You must be born anew. The wind blows
> where it wills, and you hear the sound
> of it, but you do not know <u>whence</u> it
> comes or <u>whither</u> it goes; so it is with
> every one who is born of the Spirit.
> (Jn. 3:7-8)

With these words Jesus makes clear that we do not control God's Spirit; nevertheless, we can and do observe his manifestations. Surprisingly, however, certain baptismal and confirmation practices in the church have given the impression that we can and must, in fact, control God's Spirit. It will be the purpose of the following study to expose "the whence and the whither" of the various traditions of confirmation: its biblical roots, its emergence in the liturgical tradition of the early church, its medieval development, its sixteenth century reformation, its post-Reformation development, the most recent challenges to its practice, and, finally, some practical proposals for its future. New in this book will not be the simple rehearsing of the history of confirmation, for this has already been competently provided for.[1] Rather, new will be the analysis of this history from a perspective triggered by insights into its biblical roots as these have been exposed by studies relating to the so-called "charismatic renewal" which has permeated the decade of the seventies.

Pentecostalism's recent admission into ecumenical conversations has greatly enhanced our sensitivity to certain strands of biblical tradition.[2] It is precisely these strands which now seem to have a bearing on our struggle to define what the church really means by "confirmation." The rediscovery of the connection made in the New Testament between "confirmation" and the "charismata" may just be the lost key to the riddle of confirmation which has perplexed the church for so long. For if "charismata" in the broad sense are the "gifts of the Spirit" (1 Cor. 12:1-11) and the "fruits of the Spirit" (Gal. 5:22-23), can the church determine and control their "whence and whither" by a

liturgical rite such as confirmation? What is the connection between "confirmation" and the "charismata"?

Footnotes

[1]For example, Roman Catholics can turn to M.Bohen,
<u>The Mystery of Confirmation: A Theology of the Sacra-
ment</u> (New York: Herder, 1963); Lutherans can consult
Arthur C. Repp, <u>Confirmation in the Lutheran Church</u>
(St. Louis: Concordia, 1964) or Frank W. Klos, <u>Con-
firmation and First Communion</u> (Minneapolis: Augsburg,
1968); and Anglicans have Gregory Dix, <u>The Theology
of Confirmation in relation to Baptism</u> (Westminster:
Dacre, 1946); G. W. H. Lampe, <u>The Seal of the Spirit</u>
(London: SPCK, 1951/67); and K. B. Cully, ed., <u>Con-
firmation: History, Doctrine, and Practice</u> (Greenwich:
Seabury, 1962).

[2]The story of this development is given by David
J. DuPlessis, <u>The Spirit Bade Me Go</u> (rev. ed.)(Plainfield, N. J.: Logos International, 1970).

Chapter One

CONFIRMATION IN THE NEW TESTAMENT

I   Jesus' Confirmation

Jesus was baptized, but was he ever confirmed?

This would be an interesting question to try out on a confirmation instruction class, for hidden within it is the question regarding the biblical foundation for confirmation. If such a class were asked to cite the biblical basis for Christian baptism, it would quickly come up with Matt. 28:16-20 or Mk. 16:14-16. Or if asked for the biblical basis for the celebration of the Lord's Supper, it would come up with Matt. 26:26-29, and parallels, as well as with 1 Cor. 11:23-34. In fact, such a class could with a little prodding come up with a relatively clear biblical basis for confessing one's faith (Matt. 10:32-33), for the absolving of sins (Jn. 20:21-23), for diligence in prayer (Lk. 11:9-12), for laying hands on the sick (Mk. 16:18) and on newly appointed ministers (Acts 6:1-6; 13:1-3; 1 Tim. 4:13-14; 2 Tim. 1:6). But an unambiguous biblical basis for a rite of confirmation? That's a good question.

Jesus was baptized, but was he ever confirmed? Just what happened at his baptism?

This would be an appropriate question to ask an entire Christian assembly on the First Sunday after the Epiphany, now celebrated as the Festival of the Baptism of our Lord. The Gospel appointed for that day is either Matt. 3:13-17; Mk. 1:4-11; or Lk. 3:15-17, 21-22. The Epistle is Acts 10:34-38 and the Old Testament lesson is Is. 42:1-7. These lessons all conspire to say that Jesus experienced a special manifestation of or anointing with the Holy Spirit at his baptism. But does Jesus' baptism have anything at all to do with our baptism?

Contemporary research is convinced that it does, emphasizing that this connection is perhaps even more important than the traditionally cited "Great Commission."[1] At his baptism Jesus identified fully with the needs of a sinful mankind (Matt. 3:13-15). And at our baptism we are fully identified with Jesus and his saving activity on behalf of a sinful mankind (Rom.6:3-7). So the connection between his baptism and ours is mutual identification - he identifies with us and we identify (are identified) with him.

However, it would seem important also to note some differences between the effect of Jesus' baptism and ours. Many Christians teach that their baptism is the means of their being "born again." It is of interest to note that the variety of evidences for being born again mentioned in the First Letter of John (2:29; 3:9, 14; 5:1, 4, 18), all have their foundation in the being "born of water and the Spirit" of Jn. 3:5. The italicized _of_ in the King James Version of this text ("born of water and _of_ the Spirit") introduces a distortion into the text, for the Greek does not allow this second preposition and its appearance changes the meaning of the text significantly.[2] Its duplication necessitates an understanding of the verse along the following lines: "Unless one is born of water (that is, naturally) and of the Spirit (that is, supernaturally), he cannot enter the kingdom of God." But this is to do what the Greek text does not do and that is to separate the Spirit from the water. The Greek text, as well as its translation in the Revised Standard Version, connects water and the Spirit by using a single "of." The "born again" experience has its foundation and source in a single action "of water and the Spirit." That is Christian baptism. - But was _Jesus_ "born again" from a "son of man" to a "son of God" at his baptism? Here the connection between Jesus' baptism and ours hardly applies.

Although Jesus was not "born again" at his baptism and we are, something else happened at his baptism which might yet somehow be connected with ours. There was an "epiphany" - a manifestation - of his divine sonship, which "anointing" (Acts 10:38) served as a public "commissioning" (cf. 2 Cor. 1:21-22) for his messianic ministry. The text reports a visible and an audible "beholding" of something supernatural: the heavens were opened and the Spirit of God was _seen_ descending like a dove and alighting on him; a voice from heaven was _heard_ announcing that Jesus was God's beloved Son in whom he was well pleased. Luke significantly adds that these manifestations occurred not merely in connection with his baptism but while he "was praying" (Lk. 3:21-22). In other words, Jesus' obedient baptismal identification with sinful mankind released, in the context of prayer, an experiential "confirmation" from God of his good pleasure in his Son.

It would seem significant, however, that such

"confirmation" occurred not only once in his life and in connection with a ritual, but repeatedly. He was never "rebaptised" with water, but he was "reconfirmed" by means of spiritual manifestations. This would seem to have been the case at his so-called "transfiguration" (Matt. 17:1-8; Mk. 9:2-8; Lk. 9:28-36), with Luke again specifying that this happened "as he was praying." It also seemed to be the case while he was praying in Gethsemane (Matt. 26:30-35; Mk. 14:32-42;Lk.22: 39-46), with Luke reporting the appearance of "an angel from heaven, strengthening (confirming?) him" (cf. also Matt. 4:11).

Jesus was baptized, but he was also confirmed. He was "confirmed" when in faith-full and prayer-full o-bedience he acted out his previously given and established divine sonship. The Father confirmed him in this sonship by means of a variety of spiritual manifestations.

II The Apostles' Confirmation

All four Gospels relate the story of the baptism of Jesus and each of the accounts is preceded by a significant word of John the Baptist. He says:

> "I baptize you with water for repentance, but he who is coming after me is mightier than I, whose sandals I am not worthy to carry; he will baptize you with the Holy Spirit and with fire" (Matt. 3:11; cf. Mk. 1: 7-8; Lk. 3:16; Jn. 1:32-34).

Jesus was baptized and confirmed. Were the Apostles baptized? Were the Apostles confirmed? John the Baptist here prophesies that they could expect to be baptized "with the Holy Spirit and with fire." When did this happen? Are two separate baptisms predicted?

Again the Greek text has only one preposition binding Spirit and fire together, so the translation would read better as: "he will baptize you with the Holy Spirit and fire." As with John 3:5 above the question might be asked whether here too we do not have a unified event consisting now of the Holy Spirit and fire, but with the Holy Spirit expressing the internal dimension of which fire is the external manifestation. The purgative and refining effect of fire will manifest the work which the Holy Spirit is effecting internally upon the heart. And for Luke the manifestation of "tongues as of fire"(Acts 2:3) relates this fire in a positive way to the hot-tongued "utterance" which the Holy Spirit was provoking in those who had been filled with him (Acts 2:4).

What, then, was happening when on the first Pentecost the Apostles were being thus baptized "with the Holy Spirit and fire" - something which Jesus himself also predicted would happen to them, but which he referred to as the "Holy Spirit and power" rather than as the "Holy Spirit and fire" (Lk. 24:49; Acts 1:4-5, 8). Was this the point at which the Apostles were "born again"?

It would hardly seem that the Pentecost event marked the day upon which the Apostles became "children of God" (Jn. 1:12-13). Or are we actually to think of them as first coming to faith and receiving Jesus on that day? Such an interpretation would make it difficult to know what to call their relationship to Jesus when "they left their nets and followed him" (Mk. 1:17-18).[3] Were they still children of darkness when they saw the risen Lord and were "glad" (Jn. 20: 20) and returned to Jerusalem with great "joy"(Lk.24: 52)? Did Jesus bequeath them peace and his Holy Spirit and commission them with the continuation of his ministry while they were still hardened unbelievers or at best softened Old Testament believers (Jn. 20:19-23)?

In no way can Pentecost be the simple equivalent of Christian baptism for the Apostles. If baptism means "mutual identification," Jesus with us and we with Jesus (see above, p. 3), this happened for the Apostles before Pentecost. It happened initially as "they left their nets and followed him." This was their unique Christian baptism.

But, then, what happened to them on Pentecost? - This was for them a "confirmation" - a visible and audible "manifestation" of their own adoptive call as "sons of God" (Acts 2:32-33), an "anointing" and public "commissioning" for their apostolic ministry (Acts 2:22, 43). And it was repeatable (Acts 4:5-13, 23-35).

Although for the three thousand, those who on the first Pentecost received the apostolic word and were baptized, that day marked their initiation into the body of Christ (Acts 2:37-42), for the Apostles it was something different. That day marked their "confirmation," even as Jesus had promised (Acts 1:4-5, 8).

III The Believers' Confirmation

Many have heard of "believer's baptism." But
"believer's confirmation"? What's that? If we succeed in answering that question, perhaps we will also
find ourselves coming into an ecumenically satisfying
resolution of the split between sacramental baptism and
believer's baptism - that is, the split between baptism
as the _gift_ of God's grace and baptism as a _response_ to
that gift.[4]

The Pentecost account in the Book of Acts serves
as a good transition from a discussion of Jesus' confirmation and the Apostles' confirmation to a discussion of the believers' confirmation. Bible scholars
are not sure whether the number of those who were filled
with the Holy Spirit on the first Pentecost was twelve
(Acts 1:24-26; 2:14-16) or one hundred twenty (Acts 1:
14-15; 2:1). But this ambiguity serves well to signal
the fact that "confirmation" was something intended not
only for Jesus or for the twelve Apostles but also for
the entire "company of those who believed" (Acts 2:1;
4:31-32).[5]

This is the clear implication of the so-called
spurious ending of Mark's Gospel. The passage is particularly interesting since it employs the very word
"confirm" (Greek = bebaioō). Since the date of writing
is suspected of being about eighty years after the rest
of Mark's Gospel, it serves as a powerful witness from
the church of the second century that the "confirmation"
of believers was still at that point very much a part
of the church's consciousness. In this text we are
told that certain "_signs_ will accompany those who believe" (Mk. 16:17-18) and then we are told that "the
Lord worked with them ⌊the eleven - v. 14⌋ and _con-
firmed_ the message by the _signs_ that attended it"
(Mk. 16:20).

We find here the same ambiguity of numbers ("those
who believe" and "the eleven") as we found in the Acts
account. The confirmation of the Apostles is sliding
over into the confirmation of the believers. And even
though it is here the "message" which is said to be
"confirmed" (v. 20), the "signs" which do the confirming are precisely the signs which "accompany those who
believe." Thus the believers are confirmed when the
message which they believe is confirmed. It is "the
Lord" (Jesus - vv. 19-20; cf. Acts 2:32-33) who does
the confirming and he does so by manifesting spiritual
"signs" in their midst - different but similar signs

to those that attended Jesus at his baptism/confirmation and the Apostles at their Pentecostal confirmation.

That Pentecostal confirmation was not understood as being limited to the twelve Apostles is underscored by Luke in the remainder of the Book of Acts. What began in a focused, though ambiguous, way with the Apostles (Acts 2:14; 4:29-33), soon began to filter down to men like Stephen (6:8), Phillip (8:6-7), Ananias, Saul, and Barnabas (9:10-19; 13:1-12). But it would be appropriate at this point to ask what, if anything, seemed to trigger such Pentecostal confirmations?

The simple answer is obedience and prayer. It was that for Jesus, for the Apostles, and finally for all believers. When Jesus was "confirmed" by spiritual manifestations in connection with his baptism, it followed upon his obedience and prayer (Matt. 3:13-17; Lk. 3:21-22). When the Apostles were similarly confirmed on the first Pentecost, it again followed upon obedience (they "returned to Jerusalem" - Acts 1:4-5, 12) and prayer (they "with one accord devoted themselves to prayer" - Acts 1:14). Such obedience and prayer are inseparably related to faith and this trinity of human responses are all rooted and grounded in God's Word (Acts 1:4).

It is an interesting and revealing exercise to read the entire Book of Acts to determine whether confirmation via Pentecostal manifestations is consistently tied to this trinity of responses. Having made such an investigation we note the following:

Acts 4:31 - "And when they had _prayed_ . . . ."

5:32 - "to those who _obey_ him."

6:5-6, 8 - "_prayed_ for them . . . laid their hands on them . . . ."

8: 14-17 - "_prayed_ for them . . . . laid their hands on them . . . ."

9:10-19 - "he is _praying_ . . . and laying his hands on him . . . ."

10:1-2, 44-48 - "and _prayed_ constantly . . . . the Holy Spirit fell on all who <u>heard the word</u>."

11:15-17 - "when we <u>believed</u> . . . . "

12:5-17 - "<u>prayer</u> for him . . . gathered together and were <u>praying</u> . . . . "

16:25-34 - "<u>praying</u> and singing hymns . . . "

19:1-7   - "when you <u>believed</u> . . . laid his hands upon them . . . "

27:21-26;
28:1-6   - "<u>faith</u> in God . . . . "

28:7-9 -   "<u>prayed</u> and putting his hands on him . . . . "

An analysis of the foregoing reveals that Pentecostal manifestations of confirming signs are indeed tied to obedience, prayer, and faith as responses to God's Word and that it is particularly prayer which seems to trigger such manifestations.

However, the appeal to the Book of Acts as authority for what the church should be doing or expecting today has frequently been challenged by the distinction made between that which is simply <u>described</u> as history in Holy Scripture and that which is <u>prescribed</u> specifically for us.[6] For this reason it would be important to document an understanding of confirmation as found in the apostolic letters of the New Testament. The question to be answered would be: Do these letters prescribe for us (that is, for believers) such a phenomenon as "believers' confirmation"?

Investigating the New Testament Epistles with this question in mind we come up with the following:

Rom. 1:11   - "impart to you some <u>spiritual gift</u> (charisma) to <u>strengthen</u> you . . . . "

Rom. 15:18-19 - "win <u>obedience</u> . . . by word and and deed, by the power of <u>signs and wonders</u>, by the power of the Holy Spirit . . . . "

1 Cor. 1:5-7   - "the testimony to Christ was
                        confirmed among you . . . not
                        lacking in any spiritual gift
                        (charismati) . . . ."

1 Cor. 12:1-11,
31; 14:1, 12-13   - "earnestly desire the (higher,
                        spiritual) gifts . . . eager
                        for manifestations of the Spirit
                        . . . building up the church
                        . . . pray for the power . . . ."

2 Cor. 1:21-22   - "it is God who establishes
                        (confirms) us . . . and has
                        commissioned (anointed) us
                        . . . put his seal upon us and
                        given us his Spirit in our
                        hearts as a guarantee."

Gal. 3:5   - "Does he who supplies the
                        Spirit . . . miracles . . .
                        by works of the law, or by
                        hearing with faith?"

Eph. 1:13-14   - "and have believed in him, were
                        sealed with the promised Holy
                        Spirit . . . guarantee . . . ."

Eph. 4:30   - "And do not grieve the Holy
                        Spirit . . . sealed . . . ."

Eph. 5:18   - "but be [continually] filled
                        with the Spirit, addressing one
                        another . . . ."

Phil. 3:9-11   - "faith; that I may know . . .
                        power of his resurrection
                        . . . ."

Phil. 4:13   - "I can do all things in him who
                        strengthens me."

Col. 2:11-12;
Rom. 4:11   - "In him also you were circum-
                        cised . . . and you were buried
                        with him in baptism . . . . He
                        received circumcision as a sign
                        or seal . . . ."

1 Thess. 1:5   - "our gospel came to you . . .
                        word . . . power . . . . Holy
                        Spirit . . . full conviction."

1 Tim. 4:14-15 - "Do not neglect the <u>gift</u>
                 (<u>charismatos</u>) you have . . .
                 prophetic utterance . . . <u>laid</u>
                 <u>their hands</u> upon you . . . that
                 all may <u>see</u> your progress."

2 Tim. 1:6-7 - "rekindle the <u>gift (charisma)</u>
                 . . . through the <u>laying on of</u>
                 <u>my hands</u> . . . a spirit of
                 <u>power</u> . . . ."

Hebr. 2:3-4   - "it was <u>attested (confirmed)</u>
                 to us . . . while <u>God</u> also bore
                 witness by <u>signs and wonders</u>
                 <u>and various miracles and by</u>
                 <u>gifts of the Holy Spirit</u> . .
                 . . "

2 Pet. 1:3-11 - "supplement your <u>faith</u> with
                 <u>virtue</u> . . . zealous to <u>con-</u>
                 <u>firm</u> your call and election .
                 . . . "

2 Pet. 1:16-19 - "the <u>power</u> and coming . . .
                 prophetic word <u>made more sure</u>
                 (<u>bebaioteron</u>). . . rises in
                 <u>your hearts</u>."

1 Jn. 2:26-27 - "the <u>anointing</u> which you re-
                 ceived . . . abides in you .
                 . . <u>teaches</u> you about every-
                 thing . . . "

Other passages could also be adduced but this
overview should certainly be sufficient to find an
answer to our question: Do the New Testament Epistles
authorize such a phenomenon as "believers' confirmation"? We remember, of course, that the Epistles are
not systematic treatises on theology but letters com-
posed to meet specific, practical needs in young, mission congregations. Therefore the task of systematiz-
ing the mass of information given here is left to us.
To facilitate the task of systematization we shall di-
vide the above question into three components and then
analyze the Scriptural references with a view to these
subdivisions. The three components of our question
are:

1) What is the function of the "charismata"
    (manifestations of the Spirit)?

2) What provokes their appearance?

3) Are they an optional accessory to the Christian life?

A simple and by now familiar concept to describe the function of the "charismata" is the word "confirmation." The appearance of "charismata" in the life of the believer "strengthens," "seals," and "guarantees" the believer's self-understanding as a child of God and thus equips him or her to carry out the call to live the Christian life in a manner which builds up the church.

The appearance of the "charismata" is provoked by "earnest desire" and "love," that is, by prayer and zealous service. The Lord is the "confirmer," but he confirms faith expressing itself in prayer and obedience.

The "charismata" and the "confirmation" which they bring are not optional accessories to the Christian life. Although their distribution is conditioned by the Lord's good will and pleasure, he places believers under an urgent exhortation to seek such manifestations as will "confirm" their self-understanding as God's chosen ones and contribute to the building up of the body of Christ.

Accordingly, to answer our key question, the New Testament Epistles do authorize and prescribe such a phenomenon as "believers' confirmation." Baptism does not so much presuppose faith as it establishes faith by initiating the baptized into a covenant relationship with God through Christ. Confirmation, on the other hand, does presuppose faith, since it is precisely this faith which is to be confirmed by God. "Believer's baptism"? Not if thereby is meant that baptism merely signals faith rather than establishes it. "Believers' confirmation"? Yes, if thereby is meant that every believer is exhorted to have his or her faith confirmed by the manifestation of "charismata," which in turn are to be used for body-building ministry.

The mention of "covenant" in relation to baptism is suggested by Paul's association of baptism with circumcision, the sign of the covenant in the Old Testament (Col. 2:11-12). Earlier he had spoken of circumcision as a "sign or seal" of a faith born of the covenant of promise (Rom. 4:11-12; Gal. 4:21-31). Now he speaks of "the promised Holy Spirit" as "seal" and

"guarantee" of the new covenant of promise (Eph. 1:
13-14; 2:11-13; 2 Cor. 1:21-22).

Much contemporary baptismal practice short-cir-
cuits some of this intricate reasoning on the part of
the Apostle Paul. We notice this when we consider
what it is that for many serves as the "seal" and
"guarantee" of their belonging to the covenant of promise. The answer comes back, their baptism, and the
seal and guarantee of that is most manifestly their
baptismal certificate. However, that is not Paul's
point. He does not call baptism as such the seal and
guarantee, but the Holy Spirit functions thus. Baptism is a Christ-ordained and therefore dependable com-
municator of the promise, but not its seal and guarantee. The seal and guarantee are the promised Holy
Spirit received by faith.

Perhaps the point can be made still more clearly
by considering the circumcision/baptism analogy somewhat further. In the Old Testament covenant of promise, circumcision was the "seal." Can we all imagine
how humorous it would have appeared had a father asked
the priest for an official "circumcision certificate"
as "seal and guarantee" that his son had beyond all
doubt been circumcised? Nonsense. The circumcision
left its own evidence in the flesh and it was a visible seal and guarantee that one indeed had become a
participant in the covenant of promise. But, the Apostle says, it was "made in the flesh by hands" (Eph. 2:
11). Now he testifies to a circumcision "made without
hands" (Col. 2:11). Certainly this cannot refer to the
external act of baptism by itself, since that, like
circumcision, involves the use of human hands. But no
hands seal the baptized with the Holy Spirit. This
mark upon the heart is made by the Holy Spirit himself
and it is a mark which this self-same Spirit makes visible through the "charismata" which are manifestations
of his own presence (1 Cor. 12:4-11). "Confirmation"
in the New Testament is a "seal," but it is not merely
"made in the flesh _[or on the forehead]_ by hands"(cf.
Rev. 7:1-8;9:1-6). It is "made without hands" by the
Holy Spirit himself as he "confirms" the faith, which
rests in the baptismally conferred "promised Holy
Spirit," through the charismatic manifestations of the
Spirit in the obedient and praying believer. Even the
"laying on of hands" is not of itself the "seal" or
"confirmation." It is always the Holy Spirit himself
and his manifestations, while the "laying on of hands"
is only an external and optional signal of that necessary prayer for the answer to which one can only

"wait" (Acts 1:4).

Thus far we have seen that "believers' confirmation" is attested in the conclusion of Mark's Gospel, in the Book of Acts, and in the New Testament Epistles. Now we wish to see whether there is also evidence for it in the Gospel of John, which is looked upon by scholars as offering "the summit of New Testament pneumatology [doctrine of the Holy Spirit]"[7]

For a clue to John's answer to the question we are drawn to one of the concluding statements of his Gospel. He writes:

> Now Jesus did many other _signs_ in the presence of the disciples, which are not written in this book; but these are written that you may _believe_ that Jesus is the Christ, the Son of God, and that believing you may have life in his name. (Jn. 20:30-31)

These words follow directly upon Jesus' gentle rebuke directed to "doubting" Thomas, namely, "Blessed are those who have _not seen_ and _yet believe_" (Jn. 20:29). According to this, just what function do the "signs" of Jesus fulfill? Are they the foundation of faith? Or its confirmation?

The "Doubting Thomas" pericope is an important one, since it gives a summary illustration of John's answer to this question. We should first of all note that there are two kinds of doubt, namely, that of a believer and that of an unbeliever. The doubt of the unbeliever is reflected in the taunt of the chief priests and scribes recorded by Mark (15:31-32):

> He saved others; he cannot save himself. Let the Christ, the King of Israel, come down now from the cross, that we may see and believe.

Contrast this with Thomas': "Let us also go, that we may die with him" (Jn. 11:16)[8] Jesus' death shook Thomas to the core of his being. Why live, if Jesus was dead? When Thomas was confronted with the "good news" of Jesus' resurrection, it was too good to be true. His glimmering faith wanted to believe it, but that faith needed "confirmation." It needed first-hand experience that what it wanted to believe was not mere wishful thinking but objective truth. Jesus responded to Thomas differently than to the taunt of the

14

high priests and scribes. Why? "Because he knew all
men and needed no one to bear witness of man; for he
himself knew what was in man" (Jn. 2:23-25). And so
he could "trust himself" to Thomas, for Thomas truly
and deeply wanted to believe, whereas the others had
no such desire at all. In Thomas there was present a
faith - an extremely weak and faltering one, but one
which could be confirmed; in the others there was none
and to them Jesus could only give the sign of the pro-
phet Jonah (Matt. 12:38-40). Only after Jesus had lov-
ingly confirmed Thomas' faith with the personal "sign"
of his visible presence, did he also gently exhort him
to a faith which ultimately did not find its foundation
in signs. Jesus' own public ministry began after his
own dramatic "confirmation" through signs. It ended
without signs, in an experienced abandonment by God,
but with a persistent "nevertheless" trust (Mk. 15:
34-37) in his Father's word to him: "Thou art my beloved Son: with thee I am well pleased" (Mk. 1:11).
Thus Jesus could lay down his life trusting God for the
ultimate "confirmation" in the sign yet to be given in
his resurrection. The "signs" of John's Gospel are not
intended to furnish a foundation for faith. Only the
"Good News" can do that. But John does testify to the
confirming power of Jesus' signs in those who believe.

Does John understand these signs to occur as unsolicited expressions of God's sheer grace? The request of a believing Jewish mother seemed to trigger
the "first sign" (Jn. 2:1-11) and the request of a believing Gentile father, the "second sign" (Jn. 4:
46-54). Jesus urges a Samaritan woman to ask for that
water (Spirit?) which will become a "spring of water
welling up to eternal life" (Jn. 4:7-15; cf. Jn. 7:
37-39) and he promises "another Counselor" ("Confirmer"?) to those believers who keep his commandments
(Jn. 14:12-17). So from the earliest New Testament
writings to those closing out the canon there is a consistent witness that "confirmation" is given to those
who obediently and prayerfully ask for it, seek for it,
and knock for it at the door (that is, Jesus - Jn.10:
7, 9) of the Father's heart (Lk. 11:9-13).

IV Summary: The Whence and the Whither of Confirma-
            tion in the New Testament

A study of the New Testament reveals that there
is no particular "rite way," but that there is a "right
way" to look upon confirmation. That "right way"
(also called "canonical") is to understand confirmation as that which God does in response to a faith

which obediently and prayerfully seeks after God. God's "confirmation" is experienced "when you seek him with all your heart" (Jer. 29:11-14). That is a "right" which God gives to his people and which he exhorts them to exploit. Thomas was only doing what the Psalmist did before him when he prayed: "Show me a _sign_ of thy favor . . . " (Ps. 86:17).

Confirmation in the New Testament is not an unrepeatable act or rite. The fact that the New Testament uses a verbal expression such as "he _will baptize_ you with the Holy Spirit" and never "_the baptism_ with the Holy Spirit" indicates that this confirming baptism with its spiritual manifestations is necessarily understood as a repeatable event rather than as a singular, isolated, and unrepeatable rite. The verbal form of the New Testament expression would at best allow us to speak nominally of "_a baptism_ with the Holy Spirit," the indefinite article suggesting the repeatability of this "confirming" action of the Holy Spirit.

But whence, then, the reduction of New Testament "confirmation" to a rite? That will be the story of the following chapter.

Footnotes

[1]Eugene L. Brand, _Baptism: A Pastoral Perspective_ (Minneapolis: Augsburg Publishing House, 1975), pp. 15-16; Richard Jungkuntz, _The Gospel of Baptism_ (St. Louis: Concordia Publishing House, 1968), pp. 33-36; Aidan Kavanagh, _The Shape of Baptism: The Rite of Christian Initiation_ (New York: Pueblo, 1978), pp. 11; 13.

[2]A helpful discussion of Jn. 3:5 is found in the challenging study by James D. G. Dunn, _Baptism in the Holy Spirit: A Re-examination of the New Testament Teaching on the Gift of the Spirit in relation to Pentecostalism today_ (Philadelphia: The Westminster Press, 1970), pp. 183-194.

[3]Dietrich Bonhoeffer writes: "In the Synoptic Gospels the relationship between the disciples and their Lord is expressed almost entirely in terms of following him. In the Pauline Epistles this conception recedes into the background . . . . Where the Synoptic Gospels speak of Christ calling men and their following him, St. Paul speaks of _Baptism_." _The Cost of Discipleship_ (New York: The Macmillan Co., 1959),

pp. 205-206.

[4]William H. Lazareth and Nikos Nissiotis, eds.
Baptism, Eucharist and Ministry (Geneva: World Council
of Churches, 1982), pp. 2-7, documents a recent step
in that direction. See also "Lutheran-Baptist Dialogue," ed. Joseph A. Burgess and Glenn A. Igleheart,
in _American Baptist Quarterly_, Vol. I, No. 2 (Dec.,
1982), pp. 99-215.

[5]For a discussion of the number of people involved
see George T. Montague, _The Holy Spirit: Growth of a
Biblical Tradition_ (Paramus: Paulist Press, 1976),
pp. 276-277.

[6]A good treatment of this problem is that by Gor-
den D. Fee, "Hermeneutics and Historical Precedent -
A Major Problem in Pentecostal Hermeneutics," in _Per-
spectives on the New Pentecostalism_, Russell P. Spittler, ed. (Grand Rapids: Baker Book House, 1976),
pp. 118-132.

[7]Montague, op. cit., p. 333.

[8]Much of the following exposition of the "Doubting Thomas" pericope is that suggested by Helmut Thielicke, _I Believe: The Christian's Creed_ (Philadelphia:
Fortress Press, 1968), pp. 172-187.

Chapter Two

CONFIRMATION IN THE FIRST FIVE CENTURIES

In the preceding chapter we have used the word "confirmation" to refer particularly to manifestations of "charismata," the gifts and the fruit of the Spirit, whereby Jesus, the Lord, "confirms" the faith of those whom he has already called his own through Holy Baptism, when they in turn exercise that struggling faith by responding to his Word in obedience and prayer. There is a sense, however, in which that definition is a somewhat arbitrary choice - not therefore inappropriate, but in need of further clarification in the light of other New Testament possibilities. We chose to concentrate on this meaning, since it has been the most neglected even while the best attested understanding of the word "confirmation" in the New Testament. But at this point we must, before proceeding, acknowledge other and related meanings of the broader concept of "confirmation" insofar as they are allowed by the biblical witness.

The concept "confirmation" may be used in the sense of "reaffirmation," whether that be God's reaffirmation of the grace he promises to faith or whether that be the believer's reaffirmation of the faith whereby he responds to God's grace. This meaning of confirmation amounts to the repetition of a promise, whether that be God's promise to the person called to believe or whether that be the believer's promise to the God who has called him or her. Thus confirmation can mean reaffirmation, repetition, or ratification of a promise. Holy Scripture does not so much use the term in this way as it cites the practice. For instance, one again and again hears God reaffirming or repeating his covenant as made to Abraham (Gen. 17; 28); and God's backsliding people are repeatedly called upon to reaffirm their response to the Lord (2 Chron. 15).

But the word "confirm" ("stablish;" "establish") is used in Scripture in another sense, namely, that which has been described in the previous chapter. Here the sense of the word "confirm" is not merely to "reaffirm" the content of a promise, but actually to "fulfill" that promised content in one's experience. For instance, in Ps. 119:38 we hear the psalmist cry: "Confirm [that is, fulfill] to thy servant thy promise, which is for those who fear thee." The Hebrew word koom is frequently used in this sense (1 Sam. 1:23; Is. 44:26; Ezek. 13:6; Dan. 9:12), as is bebaioo in the New Testament (Rom. 15:8).

As the first century church began to live out its Lord's mandates, practices developed which corresponded to this variety of meanings for the notion of confirmation. Following prophetic and apostolic example the church developed practices whereby the Lord's promises to her could be repeatedly "reaffirmed" and whereby her promises to the Lord could also be regularly "reaffirmed." Worship centered on the use of "Word and sacraments," God's way of reaffirming his promises to his people. And his people responded by reaffirming their faith in creeds, in hymns, and in a developing liturgy and ritual. But less and less seems to be heard of what Scriptural vocabulary actually designates as confirmation in the sense of the experienced fulfillment of God's promises to his people. And more and more the "right" of God's people to expect such experiential fulfillment and confirmation of his promises is reduced to a "rite" whereby God's and the people's promises to each other are reaffirmed, but the "charismatic manifestations" are little expected or experienced. Rather than in prayerful expectancy "to wait for the promise of the Father" (Acts 1:4), we note the development of proliferating ritual which takes the place of what those in Jerusalem could "see and hear" when Jesus poured out upon his own the promised Holy Spirit (Acts 2:32-33). This history we shall now proceed to sketch and to analyze.

I   Confirmation-Chrismation in the Apostolic Church

The Apostle Paul seems to have spent much of his ministry in "confirming" (KJV) and "strengthening" (RSV) /episterizō/ the souls of the disciples (Acts 14: 22; 15:32, 41; 18:23). He did this essentially through "teaching and preaching <u>the word of the Lord</u>" (Acts 15: 35)- in other words, through reaffirming to them God's promises. But in Eph. 3:14-21 we have recorded a <u>prayer</u> in which Paul on bended knee implores the Father that "he grant /the Ephesian saints_7 to be <u>strengthened</u> /krataioō_7 with might through his Spirit in the inner man." This "strengthening" seems to come by way of "consciousness expansion," namely, "that you, being rooted and grounded in love, may have the power to comprehend with all the saints what is the <u>breadth</u> and <u>length</u> and <u>height</u> and <u>depth</u> and to know the <u>love of Christ</u> which <u>surpasses knowledge</u>, that you may be <u>filled</u> with all the <u>fulness</u> of God." On occasion Paul could use the ancient gesture of the laying on of hands as an enacted, particularized prayer, with

the confirming result that "the Holy Spirit came on
[the Ephesian disciples] ; and they spoke with tongues
and prophesied" (Acts 19:6).

In 2 Cor. 1:21f. Paul employs four expressions
which keep recurring later in the Fathers but in ways
which move away from Paul's own theologically figura-
tive use to a more ritualistic one. The four words
are: bebaiōn, chrisas, sphragisamenos, and arrabōna.
In order they mean: confirming, anointed, marked with
a seal, earnest. It certainly need be no departure
from the faith to give ritual expression to these con-
cepts. However, when the reality which is signified
is not experienced except by way of the ritual and not
by way of a subjective, personal encounter with the
presence and working of the Holy Spirit, then we know
that the church is losing its faith and its nerve,
being no longer able to "wait for the promise of the
Father," but instead substituting for such faith-full,
expectant waiting a variety of rituals which need only
to be performed in order to "guarantee" the desired
reality. Thus the divinely sovereign Holy Spirit has
supposedly come under the would-be control of the hier-
archically sovereign priest or bishop or the charisma-
tically sovereign hot-handed believer, a la Simon Magus
(Acts 8:18-24).

But that the church did early in its history develop interpretive ritual to accompany its sacramental actions is not to be criticized as such. God never
had anything against visual aids so long as they encouraged rather than displaced faith in his promises.
Since in becoming Christians the faithful in a certain
sense were becoming priests and kings (1 Pet. 2:5;
Rev. 1:6; 5:10; 20:6), they were, following Old Testament precedent, anointed for such roles. The so-called
"baptismal aorist" used in 1 Jn. 2:27 ("but the anointing which you received from him abides in you") could
readily develop into a ritual anointing with oil in
connection with baptism (cf. 1 Jn. 2:20). This may be
harmless, in fact, even helpful, as long as the oil is
not identified with the Holy Spirit himself, whose ef-
fectual presence can only be received by faith. When
faith in the promise becomes too difficult, it can appear spiritually less demanding to play ritualistic
games with water, breath, salt, hands, oil, and milk
and honey, but only the "Deceiver" wins at this game.
Only faith in God's promises (1 Jn. 5:4-5) is his match
and God has attached his promised Holy Spirit solely to
the watery event of baptism - not to the additional visual aids of oil, salt, etc. And the manifestation of

this Holy Spirit he has promised to those who "earnestly desire" it - who ask, pray, and knock for it
(1 Cor. 12:31; 14:1, 12-13; Lk. 11:9-13).

"Confirmation-<u>Chrismation</u> in the Apostolic
Church"?[1] The canonical text of Holy Scripture would
rather suggest a different hyphenation and title for
this period of history, namely, "Confirmation-<u>Petition</u>
in the Apostolic Church."

II Confirmation-Chrismation in the Pre-Nicene Church

The text of Holy Scripture might not make a strong
case for confirmation-chrismation, but an early liturgical tradition, in some of its main elements supposedly older than the New Testament Scriptures and regarded by some as having an "Apostolic" authority of its
own independent of them, might.[2] The fullest early
description of a "confirmation rite" is given in the
<u>Apostolic Tradition</u> of Hippolytus. The rite described
by him represents the Roman tradition of about the year
215, though his great love for ancient practices might
mean that his description reaches rather far back in
time. That it represents Apostolic practice, however,
is all but out of the question.[3] Following a three-
year catechumenate and a ritually complex ceremony of
baptism at the Easter Vigil, Hippolytus reports a continuation of the baptismal rite according to the following directions:

1. And the Bishop shall lay his hand upon them
    invoking and saying:

    "O Lord God, who didst count these [Thy ser-
    vants] worthy of deserving the forgiveness
    of sins by the laver of regeneration, <u>make
    them worthy to be filled with the Holy Spirit</u>
    and send upon them Thy grace, that they may
    serve Thee according to Thy will; for to Thee
    is the glory, to the Father and to the Son
    with the Holy Ghost in the Holy Church, both
    now and forever world without end. Amen."

2. After this pouring the consecrated oil [from
    his hand] and laying his hand on his head he
    shall say:

    "I anoint thee with the holy oil in God the
    Father Almighty and Christ Jesus and the
    Holy Spirit."

3. And sealing [sphragizein] him on the forehead,
   he shall give him the kiss [of peace] and say:

   "The Lord be with you."

   And he who has been sealed shall say:

   "And with thy spirit."

4. And so he shall do to each one severally.

5. Thenceforth they shall pray together with all
   the people. But they shall not previously
   pray with the faithful before they have under-
   gone all these things.

6. And after the prayers, let them give the kiss
   of peace. And thereupon follows the celebration of the Easter Eucharist.[4]

Unfortunately there is no consistent textual witness to this version of the Apostolic Tradition. Another version renders point one above as follows:

   "O Lord God, who hast made them worthy to obtain remission of sins through the laver of
   regeneration of the Holy Spirit, send into
   them thy grace . . . ."[5]

A noting of the words we have highlighted will indicate
that whereas the former version reveals the beginning
of a separation between the effect of water baptism and
that of the anointing with oil and the consignation,
the latter version relates the effective working of the
Holy Spirit unequivocably to the washing of Holy Baptism. Accordingly it is altogether impossible to appeal to the Apostolic Tradition as an authoritative
source reaching behind the canonical Scriptures for
evidence of a "rite of confirmation" which would super-
sede the New Testament's own understanding of "confirmation," namely, "confirmation-petition" and not "confirmation-chrismation." That is, confirmation occurs
in connection with prayerful (and repeatable) waiting
for the promise of the Father and not in any restricted
sense in connection with anointings or signings or even
layings on of hands when these are ritualistically con-
ceived.

Working backwards now from the Apostolic Tradition
we come to Tertullian (c. 160 - c.220). He does not
hesitate to speak of what appears to be a sequence of
rites: baptism, anointing, signing, the imposition of

hands, and communion. He risks the startling statement, "Not that we obtain the Spirit in the water, but that cleansed in the water under the angel we are prepared for the Holy Spirit."[6] Although the single anointing which he mentions seems to belong to the baptism rather than to the laying on of hands, his division of the baptismal rite into two parts and the association of the gift of the Spirit with the second part has provided the basis for much subsequent theological discussion. This is also true of his rather disparaging remarks regarding the baptism of infants and his designation of baptism as "seal," namely, the sealing of the professed faith of the convert.[7] As in the case of the <u>Apostolic Tradition</u> we have here no unambiguous case for a distinct sacramental "confirmation-chrismation."

Another step back from the <u>Apostolic Tradition</u> brings us to Irenaeus (c.130-c.200). He has been cited both as favoring a confirmation-chrismation rite and as non-committal regarding it.[8] Whichever way one interprets the evidence, it is important to remember that Irenaeus gives clear testimony to the bestowal of the Holy Spirit through water baptism and only ambiguous evidence for any accompanying rites as means of "confirmation."

Theophilus of Antioch (115-168 or 181) seems to pick up on something which Luke reports regarding the self-same Antioch, namely, that there "the disciples were first called Christians" (Acts 11:26). He explains to a pagan friend that their name derived from an anointing with the "oil of God" (Christians = anointed ones). Again the commentators are disagreed as to whether this anointing is one literally performed with oil or merely a metaphorical reference to the anointing with the Holy Spirit at baptism, but they are all but agreed that such an anointing would in any event belong to a rite of baptism rather than to an isolated <u>rite</u> of confirmation.[9]

Justin Martyr (c.100-c.165) says nothing to destroy the ambiguity of the possible evidence marshalled to establish a pre-Nicene "confirmation-chrismation" rite. Scholars debate the evidence, but no convincing case can be made.[10] This is no accident, since the Fathers were biblical scholars and the Scriptures admit of no unambiguous evidence for any such isolated rite. Accordingly, Fathers like Clement of Alexandria (c.150-c.215), Origen (c.185-c.254), and Cyprian (c.200-c.258) also reflect the same ambiguity.[11]

But were there any circumstances arising at this
time which could have contributed to the development
of a less ambiguous and more sharply distinguishable
rite of "confirmation-chrismation"?

III Confirmation-Chrismation in the Post-Nicene Church

Every student of church history is familiar with
the fact that the conversion of the emperor Constantine
brought with it far-reaching consequences. Two such
consequences which touch upon our concern were the rap-
id growth and enculturation of the Church and along
with it the increasing regularization of the practice
of infant baptism.[12] This circumstance was bound
sooner or later to cause a development of baptismal
practices which, though possibly consistent with the
New Testament doctrine of baptism, would necessarily
have to forge ahead in finding new ways to explicate
this doctrine in the midst of changed circumstances.
The task of developing such forms as would be appropriate to the new situation was risky but unavoidable.
It was risky, because any possible misunderstanding
of the New Testament doctrine of baptism and the Holy
Spirit could then be easily projected in magnified
form in the newly developing practices. On the other
hand, it was unavoidable, because the New Testament
doctrine of baptism, which was not explicitly pro-
scriptive of infant baptism (and which, in fact, was
in some ways by implication prescriptive of it), could,
nevertheless, not be completely expressed by way of it.
The fulness of the New Testament doctrine of baptism
and the Holy Spirit could at best be expressed only
after a child had reached the age of discretion and
could therefore give a more individual, responsible,
personal, and mature response to the covenant relationship established by baptism. The development of a rite
of "confirmation," distinguishable but hardly separable
from the rite of baptism, was related to this process.

It is at this point that the designation "confirmation-chrismation" for this rite becomes even less
appropriate. "Chrismation," that is, the rite of a-
nointing with oil as an expression of the gift of the
Holy Spirit and therefore of "confirmation," becomes
more characteristic of the church in the East, whereas
in the West "confirmation" begins to take on a meaning
more readily associated with the "laying on of hands,"
namely, the blessing and commissioning of those who
had been baptized in infancy.[13] Without in any way

trying here to outline this development as it occurred
in the midst of what has been called "the tangled and
confused history of the doctrine of the baptismal gift
of the Spirit during the age of the Fathers,"[14] we call
attention yet to Augustine's (354-430) theology of baptism and the gift of the Holy Spirit as representative.

Augustine is to be counted among those many Fathers who saw in baptism, as New Testament antitype,
the real fulfillment of circumcision, the Old Testament type. This understanding places him in the context of those who interpret baptism in terms of a covenant theology and it helps to explain his notion of
this sacrament as the "sacrament of faith."[15] He insists that baptismal regeneration cannot be isolated
from the believer's reception of the Holy Spirit and
he distinguishes water and Spirit as the outward and
inward parts of a single sacrament.[16] Nevertheless,
he also suggests a conception of partial and fuller
bestowals of the Spirit. There is a partial gift in
baptism for "the forgiveness of sins" (see the Nicene
Creed), while the perfect bestowal in the form of
"charity" is reserved until later and occurs in connection with the laying on of hands. Here "charity" re-
places the "miracles and tongues" in which the opera-
tion of the Spirit was formerly manifested. The laying
on of hands is regarded primarily as the sign of incor-
poration into a fellowship. Unlike baptism but like
prayer, it is repeatable.[17]

Chrismation, on the other hand, Augustine understands qualifiedly as a "sacrament" distinct from baptism. He calls the visible oil the "sign," whereas the
invisible oil, the Holy Spirit himself, is called the
"sacrament."[18] The rite signifies entry into membership in Christ's Body by symbolizing the sharing in his
royal and priestly status.[19] Nevertheless, it serves
Augustine's anti-Donatist bias to argue that baptism
itself constitutes the "seal" by which the baptized is
stamped with an indelible character, whereas this
seal's blessing is merely stirred up through the imposition of hands upon the person who has received his
baptism within a schismatic fellowship.[20] This same
polemic is at work when he claims for the use of the
Name of God in the consecratory rites an efficacy which
cannot be destroyed even when pronounced by the unwor-
thy.[21]

Finally, Augustine places great emphasis upon the
use of the "sign of the cross." Without it the baptismal rites are incomplete. He associates this sign

with the original blood symbolism of the Passover, but
not in a way dissociated from baptism. The fundamental idea is that the sign of the cross betokens the
bearer's status as Christ's own property and it serves
as an effective prophylactic against the assaults of
the enemy.[22]

In summary, one sees in Augustine a prominent representative of the uncertainty arising in the church's
understanding of baptism in its relation to accompanying rites such as chrismation, the laying on of hands,
and the consignation. If clarity would not come soon,
the church was in grave danger of losing the certainty
of the grace of baptism amidst a plethora of competing
rites - competing because the tendency was growing
stronger to interpret these rites as having a value
independent of baptism and oriented toward the recip-
ient's sanctification rather than growing out of his
baptismal justification. The story of confirmation in
the Medieval Church will reveal whether or not the
ship of the church navigated these treacherous shoals
successfully.

Footnotes

[1]This designation has been promoted by Casimir
Kucharek, The Sacramental Mysteries: A Byzantine Approach (Allendale, N.J.: Alleluia Press, 1976), pp.124;
135; 143.

[2]This disputable point is argued by Dom Gregory
Dix, The Theology of Confirmation in relation to Baptism (Westminster: Dacre Press, 1946), p. 11.

[3]An extensive treatment of this important document is to be found in G.W.H. Lampe, The Seal of the
Spirit (London: SPCK, 1951, 1967), pp. 128-142, and
also in Leonel L. Mitchell, Baptismal Anointing
(London: SPCK, 1966), pp. 1-9.

[4]The above Hippolytan scheme is found in Dix, op.
cit., pp. 12-13. Also in Marian Bohen, The Mystery of
Confirmation: A Theology of the Sacrament (New York:
Herder and Herder, 1963), pp. 109-110, and in E.C.
Whitaker, Documents of the Baptismal Liturgy (London:
SPCK, 1960), pp. 2-7.

[5]Leonel L. Mitchell, op. cit., p. 3, and G.W.H.
Lampe, op. cit., pp. 139-141.

[6]Leonel L. Mitchell, op. cit., pp. 11.

[7]Paul K. Jewett, Infant Baptism and the Covenant of Grace (Grand Rapids: William B. Eerdmans, 1978), pp. 20-22; Lampe, op. cit., pp. 157-159.

[8]Lampe, op. cit., pp. 116-120; Kucharek, op. cit., p. 135; L.L.Mitchell, op. cit., pp. 12-13.

[9]Lampe, op. cit., p. 114; Kucharek, op. cit., pp. 135-136; L.L. Mitchell, op. cit., pp. 12-13.

[10]Leonel L. Mitchell, op. cit., pp. 13-15; Lampe, op. cit., pp. 109-111.

[11]Lampe, op. cit., pp. 153-157; 167-170; 170-178.

[12]Robert M. Grant, "Development of the Christian Catechumenate," in Made, Not Born: New Perspectives on Christian Initiation and the Catechumenate (Notre Dame: The University of Notre Dame Press, 1976), pp. 36-39; Lampe, op. cit., p. 171; Kucharek, op. cit., pp. 152-153.

[13]Lampe, op. cit., pp. 220-222; 227-231.

[14]Ibid., pp. 230-231.

[15]Ibid., pp. 85; 245-246; Jewett, op. cit., pp. 177-178.

[16]Lampe, op. cit., p. 206.

[17]Ibid., pp. 210; 229.

[18]Leonel L. Mitchell, op. cit., pp. 83-84.

[19]Lampe, op. cit., pp. 218-221.

[20]Ibid., pp. 242-243.

[21]Ibid., p. 288.

[22]Ibid., pp. 264; 266; 268f.

Chapter Three

CONFIRMATION IN THE MEDIEVAL CHURCH (500-1500)

We have noted that in the early centuries of the church's history, a variety of motifs emerged which in one way or another have been related to what many Christians have come to call "confirmation." Even though we in our day are familiar with this word as a relatively fixed term designating a particular ecclesiastical rite with a spectrum of meanings, this possibility was relatively slow in developing. The choice of this term as an appropriate one to be applied to that part of the initiatory rite now called "confirmation" is clouded with ambiguity. Does the word in this context mean "completion" (in the specific sense of supplying what is altogether lacking) or "strengthening" (whether by way of <u>stirring</u> up what is already present, or by <u>adding something new</u> to that which is already present, or by <u>fulfilling experientially</u> what is already present by way of promise)?[1]

The theologians of the medieval period seem to become growingly aware of this inherited ambiguity and so they strive to express with increasing clarity a precise meaning of "confirmation." Since they did not, however, break through to its "experiential" definition as expressed in the New Testament, but rather tended to take certain suggestive elements of the New Testament witness as were preserved in tradition, turn them into normative rituals, and finally into canonical sacraments, the genuinely New Testament relationship between confirmation and the manifestation of charismata was here not sufficiently recognized. That does not imply, however, that the experience of charismata was totally lost, but only that this experience was not related to "confirmation" and that it was generally a hit and miss affair.[2]

In the following we shall note the growing clarification of the meaning of confirmation during the medieval period, even though this clarification fell short of the fulness of the New Testament witness.

I Confirmation in the Early Middle Ages

Doctrinal development within the Early Middle Ages is perhaps best summed up in the "Sentences" of Peter Lombard (c.1100-1160) and the "Decretal" of Gratian (dec. c.1179). From the "Sentences" one can glean the

following points in reference to an accepted understanding of confirmation:

1) The anointing with oil upon the forehead was
   to be understood as the "completion" (<u>perfec-
   tio</u>) of baptism.

2) Only bishops were authorized to carry out this
   rite.

3) Through it the grace of forgiveness granted in
   baptism was supplemented by "the gift of the
   Holy Spirit for strength."

4) It is therefore the sacrament of growth and
   increased strength.

5) Like baptism and ordination it is unrepeatable.[3]

The "Decretal" of Gratian makes approximately the
same points and like the "Sentences" appeals for support not to the New Testament or even to the early Fathers, but instead to theologians like Rabanus Maurus
(c.776-856) and Hugh of St. Victor (c.1096-1141). In
addition the "Decretal" also cites as decisive authority
the so-called "Pseudo-Isidorian Decretals." The latter
contain some specific interpretations of "confirmation"
which were extremely determinative in shaping subsequent
theology and practice and yet these very "Decretals" do
not stem from the authentic Isidore, Bishop of Seville
from 600 to 636, but from an unknown compiler, pseudo-
Isidore, in about the year 850. What he attributes to
popes of the pre-Nicene Church are really theological
developments of a much later date. The following is a
brief summary of important points made relative to confirmation in this spurious but influential document.

1) All the faithful must through episcopal imposition of the hand receive the Holy Spirit after
   baptism, so that they may be full Christians,
   because when the Holy Spirit is poured into a
   man, the faithful heart is enlarged so as to
   express prudence and constancy.

2) Although baptism and confirmation are both great
   sacraments and normally not to be separated from
   one another, the latter is worthy of greater
   veneration because it can be performed only by
   a bishop and not by a lesser minister.

3) In baptism we are regenerated to life, after

baptism we are confirmed to combat. In baptism
we are washed, after baptism we are strengthened.

4) All heretics, who by the grace of God are converted after they have been baptized, must be
   reconciled with the church by the imposition of
   the hand. This sacrament of the laying on of
   the hand cannot be performed by any other than
   the bishops.[4]

According to this assessment, confirmation is not
merely a subsequent "ratification" of what has already
been granted through baptism, but it is an additional
and unique "strengthening" for life's battles, communicated exclusively through the hands of the bishop. It
was a particular intention of the "False Decretals" to
insure the bishops their discrete prerogatives and reference to the rite of confirmation isolated one such
special privilege which enhanced the bishop's authority.[5]

New, of course, is not the bishop's special involvement with confirmation. But such special prero-
gative was heightened and complicated by the growing
separation between baptism and confirmation, for this
meant that baptisms could be more generally and simply
performed by the more readily available priests, whereas confirmation demanded the special participation of
a bishop, and if one was not readily available, confirmation was postponed until such a felicitous occasion should arise. To insure that such occasions would
not be too few and far between, the Council of Meaux
(845) found it necessary to denounce in the strongest
possible terms the "damnable negligence" of certain
bishops who rarely, if ever, visited the people committed to their charge.[6] But it was such negligence,
whether intentional or whether circumstantially unavoidable, which provoked the stretching out of the interval between baptism and a rite of confirmation and
finally necessitated a theological rationale for what,
with less shame, could be considered the inexpediency
of the confirmation of infants.[7]

But the stretching out of this interval from perhaps less than one hour to perhaps more than seven
years was mediated and prepared for by a practice which
stipulated an interval of seven days. It was Alcuin
(c.735-804) and his disciple Rabanus Maurus who began
to theologize on the significance of a confirmation
prayer invoking the "Spirit of sevenfold grace." The

entrance of this expression into the theological discussion is said to have "given wings to the creative phantasy with which the theologians gave expression to the effect of confirmation."[8] In the rite of Alcuin and Rabanus the bishop laid his hand upon the baptized not immediately after the mass of the Paschal vigil, but seven days later, on so-called "Low Sunday" or "White Sunday." During the Easter octave those who had been baptized in the holy night of the Pascha wore their white robes, assisting at mass and being communicated each morning. Then on "Low Sunday" they were confirmed by the bishop and therewith laid aside their white robes in a gesture which brought to ritual expression an emerging emphasis in the rite of confirmation, namely, preparation for living the Christ-like life in a hostile world. One is reminded of the disappearance of Jesus' transfigured appearance before his descent from the mountain and the resumption of his messianic ministry (Matt. 17:1-23). At any rate, the seven day interval between baptism and episcopal confirmation as provided for in this rite, helped to prepare the mind of the Church for that complete severance of confirmation from baptism which was already in the making.

Such a severance of confirmation from baptism brought other consequences with it as well, particularly in the relationship of confirmation to eucharistic communion. Whereas early practice had seen the initiation rite climax in the neophyte's first communion, deferred confirmation now allowed for first communion before confirmation. This, of course, did not necessarily imply an earlier age for communion than had been custom, since it had been granted together with baptism and chrismation even to infants as early as the days of Cyprian (c.251).[9] But as baptism and confirmation slowly became two discrete sacraments, not only was confirmation moved from a position before communion to a position after it, but first communion itself was frequently delayed until children reached the age of discretion. The fourth Council of the Lateran (1215) ordered all who had attained this age not only to communicate for the first time but also to make their first confession.[10]

The "military motif" which was so pronounced in the "False Decretals" was something which Rabanus Maurus had stimulated and which three hundred years later Hugh of St. Victor consolidated with his view of confirmation as a sort of "youth dedication."[11] The 13th century ceremonial development of the "alapa" in

connection with confirmation (Pontifical of Durandus),
that is, the light blow delivered by the bishop on the
cheek of the confirmed, was perhaps an imitation of the
blow with the sword by which a young Teutonic warrior
was dubbed a knight. Thus it would symbolize the spiritual warfare which lay ahead for the youth submitting
to confirmation. At any rate, the "military" dimension
which was being emphasized in connection with confirmation at this time seems to have been related to the contemporary "crusader spirit" as well as to the early
church call to be ready for persecution.

In spite of the growing importance of confirmation
relative to baptism, there was one thing which even the
medieval theologians refused to do and that was to
state the necessity of confirmation in the same uncom-
promising terms which they chose to apply to baptism.
"Negligence" of confirmation, however, was indefensi-
ble, since with it "salvation can scarcely be obtained"
(Peter of Poitiers - dec.1205).[12]

II   Confirmation in the High Middle Ages

The almost 300 years between the Decretal of Gratian (c.1150) and the Council of Florence (1439) are
looked upon as the High Middle Ages with the dominating
figure being the Dominican philosopher and theologian,
Thomas of Aquinas (c.1225-74). Thomas departed from
earlier opinions about the authoritative institution of
the rite of confirmation by tracing it back to Christ -
though not to a direct _act_ of Christ, but to a _promise_
given by him, namely, Jn. 16:7. Thomas' Franciscan
friend, St. Bonaventure (1221-74), had derived confirmation from an institution by the Apostles, whereas
Bonaventure's teacher, Alexander of Hales (c.1170-1245),
had credited the Council of Meaux (845) with its institution, this occurring, of course, under the guidance
of the Holy Spirit.[13] One can sympathize, then, with
Thomas' difficulty in finding New Testament evidence
for the use of chrism by Christ. However, instead of
drawing the consequence that in the New Testament the
Holy Spirit himself is the chrism, Thomas capitulated
to the tendency of many centuries now and allowed confirmation to become one of seven sacraments, though
Christ communicated the "form" of confirmation to the
apostles without the use of a sacramental "sign."[14] It
apparently did not occur to Thomas that this omission
on Christ's part was intentional, since Christ intended
the actual manifestations of the Holy Spirit in the life
of the believer to be the sacramental "sign" of the

Spirit's presence, whereas the rituals developing in the church's practice could at best stir one's faith to believe what Christ had promised. But Thomas is to be appreciated for having drawn the attention of the church back to the historical Christ and his promise regarding the Holy Spirit.

Another plus for Thomas was his anticipation of contemporary "developmental" thinking. Using the anthropological model, according to which the acts of a child mature into acts appropriate to adulthood, Thomas argues that the power given by "baptismal character" corresponds to spiritual childhood, while the "character of confirmation" pertains to spiritual maturity.[15] Unfortunately Thomas failed to understand "spiritual adulthood" as something consistently related to psychological development. On the one hand he could simply ascribe it to the sacrament's limitless transforming power of grace, unrelated to the human conditions of age or perception; on the other hand he could use Christ for his theological model, who although he was "full of grace and truth" from the first instant of his conception, nevertheless did not manifest that fulness within himself publicly until much later at the occasion of his baptism by John in the Jordan.[16] And the reality of the incarnation demanded that it could not be. Thus Thomas appears to be torn between interpreting the inherited tradition and giving adequate expression to the developmental insight which was forcing itself upon his brilliant mind.

According to Thomas, then, baptism gives "justifying grace," whereas confirmation affords "fulness of grace." This fulness, however, has its point in that it particularly affects the relationship of the confirmand to the world outside himself, whereas baptismal grace is concentrated upon the individual's own salvation.[17] Thus confirmation has a social dimension, equipping its recipients for greater participation in the "liturgical community" and in the ranks of those who share in wearing the sign of their king's cross upon their foreheads. The confirmand's sponsors, then, naturally participate in the task of preparing these younger "spiritual knights" for the heavier battles into which they plan to follow their Lord. The Jesus into whom they were baptized is now "confirming" them and leading them forward into the battles symbolized by the wilderness and the road to Jerusalem.

Perhaps we should see this development of the "military motif" in reference to confirmation against

the backdrop of one of the pressing concerns of the
church at that time. The Albigenses (also known as
Cathari) were a heretical sect active between the 11th
and 14th centuries. They accused the Catholic Church
of interpreting literally what were really New Testament allegories and of thus "thingafying" spiritual
realities. Rejecting the sacraments they urged instead
what was called the "consolamentum," that is, "baptism
of the Holy Spirit by the imposition of hands" together
with all manner of attending rigors, even a form of
suicide by starvation called "endura." The heroism
manifest by the sectarians called forth a comparable
heroism from the orthodox and the developing rite of
confirmation afforded an appropriate occasion to bring
it to expression. The "occasion" did not thus create
a new meaning for confirmation, but it elicited and emphasized a meaning which had long been associated with
the rite, especially in terms of the "consignation."[18]

   The Waldensians (c.1200) imitated the Albigenses
in their critique of what can now be called the Roman
Catholic sacrament of confirmation, although the critique was aimed particularly at the neglect of catechization. They reintroduced the practice of the laying
on of hands (which had by this time been almost entirely displaced by the consignation even in the West), a
practice which marked the conclusion of a period of
catechetical instruction. Thus the Waldensians were
the actual initiators of what is now recognized as
"catechetical confirmation," a form of confirmation
which, however, was not yet at this point a rejection
of the sacramental understanding.[19]

   John Wycliffe (c.1329-84) and John Huss (c.1369-
1415) represent additional outspoken and influential
critics of sacramental confirmation. Their growing
appreciation for biblical authority prompted them to
question whether such a sacramental understanding could
be grounded in biblical revelation and whether the all
but absolute identification between symbol and reality
in the ritual did justice to the biblical witness regarding the Holy Spirit. They could also appeal to
Augustine for their sharper distinction between symbol
and reality. The Roman Catholic Church, on the other
hand, required that any Waldensian, Wycliffite, or
Hussite who might desire to return to the Catholic
faith, would first have to give assurances of having
accepted the salvific efficacy of confirmation.[20]

   There was, however, another front on which the
Church of Rome had to do battle and that was with the

adherents of the practice of the Eastern Church relative to confirmation. In the East chrismation-confirmation came to be sacramentally understood, but not as a sacrament to be exclusively administered by bishops, the bishops' part being confined to the blessing of the chrism (muron).[21] The Western practice was summarized in the canons of the Council of Florence (1439), where the now traditional seven sacraments were discussed and the privilege of bishops in regard to confirmation clearly laid down. For a period of time after the Council of Trent (1545-63) theologians even asked whether confirmation by a priest in the East was valid.[22] At any rate, the High Middle Ages are characterized by this growing clarity of confessional position and the drawing of a clearer line between it and any contending positions.

III Confirmation Revitalization Attempts in the Late
    Middle Ages

        It is clear that during the last one hundred years of the High Middle Ages the winds of change were gathering strength. The following one hundred years would see those winds develop into a full-blown attempt at reformation in the Church. But before gale force was reached in Luther and the subsequent Protestant Reformation, two other preliminary gusts must be noted, that arising around the so-called Bohemian Brethren and that centered in the Christian humanist, Erasmus of Rotterdam.

        The Bohemian Brethren emerged out of the Utraquist movement about 1467. Besides their insistence upon communion under the forms of both the bread and the wine, they rejected oaths and military service, depreciated town life and private property, stressed Christian discipline, and stood for a simple, pure, and unworldly Christianity. They understood baptism as efficacious for salvation only when a person spoke a personal yes to it, infant baptism being inefficacious in itself and in need of some sort of completion. Accordingly they developed (1468) a rite of confirmation which looked as follow:

    1) The maturing child is introduced to the congregation together with its godparents.

    2) The godparents testify to their having given the child consistent instruction in the faith confessed at his baptism.

3) The child is examined to determine whether it
   has accepted the Christian faith and it is
   thereupon asked whether it intends to remain
   faithful to its baptismal confession and to
   apostolic doctrine.

4) If it answers in the affirmative, the child is
   confirmed in its confession by the laying on
   of hands and the congregation unites in prayer
   for the child that it have the strength to remain faithful.

5) The child is then received fully into the congregation and is admitted to the communion at
   the Lord's Table.[23]

It has been assumed that there is at work in this
confirmation practice of the Bohemian Brethren an expression of the rationalism found otherwise in the sacramental understanding of Bohemian humanism, and that
it eventually was one of the sources which nurtured the
developing theology of the reform-minded but peace-
loving Erasmus to whom we must now turn as a key figure
of the period.[24]

Erasmus (c.1466-1536) died rejected both by Popes
at Rome and by leading Reformers among the Protestants.
His followers on both sides of the confessional struggle were being sent "by the Catholics to the stake and
by the Protestants to the block."[25] But his influence
upon Christendom remains considerable and this also in
reference to an understanding of the rite of confirmation.

He locates a point of contact for confirmation in
the monk's vow. In his famous _Praise of Folly_ (1509)
Erasmus delivers himself of a bitter satire on monas-
ticism and the corruptions of the Church, thus helping
to prepare the way for the Reformation. In the place
of monastic vows, which affect relatively few, he urges
the renewal of the baptismal vow as an obligation affecting anyone who has been baptized. At the age of
puberty the rite of baptism should be "re-enacted," not
in the sense of a repetition of baptism, but in the
sense of a personal dedication to the vows once spoken
at baptism. Yet, so enthusiastically did he emphasize
the necessity for such a "re-enactment" that one commentator has called him the only "Anabaptist" of the sixteenth century, seeing that the thousands called by
that name in reality insisted that there was actually
only one baptism, that granted to confessing believers,

whereas Erasmus engaged in real "Anabaptist" activity
by his merely verbal distinction between "repetition"
and "re-enactment" and by his ambiguous claim that what
he advocated was no more repetition of baptism than was
daily sprinkling with holy water.[26]   But word-play a-
side, Erasmus ascribed to the renewal of the baptismal
vow in connection with confirmation such an importance,
that one can speak of something new at work here in the
conception of confirmation.

New was certainly not catechetical instruction and
its ethical implications as such, which, of course, had
its ups and downs since the early church; but it was
Erasmus' modernization of the ancient practice such
that what had earlier been more closely tied to sacramental rituals was here interpreted more as an act
dealing with a kind of threefold personal response -
that of the mind, the will, and the emotions.[27] Humanist sensitivities were here being incorporated into a
traditional practice and in the process these were
somewhat transforming that practice. It was Erasmus'
way of being both a traditional "Catholic," for he did
not reject outright the sacramental understanding of
confirmation, and a modern "humanist," for the new
emphasis on the involvement of the individual's person-
hood was just that.

This brought responses for Erasmus from both the
right and the left. His Catholic opponents, especially those among the Spanish mendicant monks, accused him
of inventing a new sacrament, whereas the Anabaptist
party affirmed the qualifications which Erasmus had expressed relative to infant baptism and they appealed to
his confirmation practice as supporting their own practice of adult believer's baptism.[28]

An important dimension of Erasmus' concept of confirmation was the confidence he placed in it as God's
chosen instrument for the renewal of the church. He
had an almost naive optimism regarding the ability of
a confirmation practice reformed according to his i-
deals to move a secularized church into renewal. Humanistic ideals depended little, of course, upon God's
sovereign Spirit, but had great confidence in man's
ability to make things happen - now not by using the
heteronomous methods of the Inquisition but by appeal-
ind to the highest instincts of man's autonomous spirit.[29]

IV Summary: The Whence and the Whither of Confirma-
    tion in the Medieval Church

     We have noted above how the first five centuries
of the church's history did not succeed in bringing
great clarity to the doctrine of the baptismal gift of
the Spirit. As the rites surrounding baptism prolifer-
ated and began to take on more and more independent
value, the relationship of one rite to the other and of
all the rites to baptism itself became more tenuous.
There was a tendency for these rites to come into com-
petition with one another and finally to compete with
the justifying grace of baptism itself. In the present
chapter we have attempted to discover how the Medieval
Church dealt with this situation and to do so we have
had to concentrate upon the history of confirmation as
it developed during this 1000 year period.

     We have seen how the growing sacramentalism of the
rites accompanying baptism allowed for a more decisive
separation of baptism and confirmation and how confirmation as an independent rite could then be reinter-
preted with greater sensitivity to the changing historical situation. The perceived pastoral need to under-
score episcopal authority afforded the occasion for
limiting the performance of confirmation to the bishops.
The failure of bishops consistently to carry out their
prerogatives led to the stretching out of the interval
between baptism and confirmation, sometimes even beyond
seven or ten years. The "military motif" already found
in the baptismal understanding of the early church was
further elicited and developed in response to the cru-
sading spirit and knightly ideal of the contemporary
culture. And finally the humanistic impulse to protect
and save a threatened Christian culture through a movement of mass education rather than by the force of the
sword or the thumbscrew, and to draw upon the power la-
tent in the developing self-consciousness of the human
personality rather than upon the impersonal authority
of traditional conformism, gave birth to a new model
for confirmation - the catechetical. Medieval Chris-
tianity had progressively sharpened the interpretation
and practice of confirmation in the direction of an
independent sacrament - even a superior sacrament -
with the result that this over-sacramentalizing of a
rite which actually had its taproot in faith-full prayer and obedience as the necessary response to baptismal
grace, brought with it a reaction expressing itself in
a growing depreciation of sacramental grace and a growing confidence in personal decisions and ethical com-
mitments.

Would this newly developing foundation for confirmation provide the rock upon which the rain, the floods,
and the winds (Matt.7:24-27) of the sixteenth century
Protestant Reformation could beat without destroying
that sacrament?

Footnotes

[1]See the helpful appendix tracing the use of the
words "confirmare" and "confirmatio" in J.D.C. Fisher,
<u>Christian Initiation: Baptism in the Medieval West</u>
(London: SPCK, 1965), pp. 141-148.

[2]Some helpful cues along this line are found in
the essay by E. Glenn Hinson entitled "A Brief History
of Glossolalia" in the book co-authored by Frank Stagg,
E. Glenn Hinson, Wayne E. Oates, <u>Glossolalia: Tongue
Speaking in Biblical, Historical, and Psychological
Perspective</u> (Nashville: Abingdon, 1967), pp.47-58; also
in the essay by Jean Laporte entitled "The Holy Spirit,
Source of Life and Activity According to the Early
Church" in the book edited by Edward D. O'Conner,
<u>Perspectives on Charismatic Renewal</u> (Notre Dame: Uni-
versity of Notre Dame Press, 1975), pp.88-89; and finally in Judith Tydings, <u>Gathering a People: Catholic
Saints in Charismatic Perspective</u> (Plainfield, N.J.:
Logos International, 1977), pp.148; 162-163. Nevertheless, the memory of a relationship between confirmation
and the charismata is found in what has been called the
"curious connection" between confirmation and the working of miracles made by Paschasius (d.512). See Lampe,
op. cit., p.302.

[3]A helpful summary and interpretation of the history of confirmation in the Middle Ages is included in
the essay by Wilhelm Maurer entitled "Geschichte von
Firmung und Konfirmation bis zum Ausgang der lutherischen Orthodoxie" in the book edited by Kurt Frör,
<u>Confirmatio: Forschungen zur Geschichte und Praxis der
Konfirmation</u> (München:Evang. Presseverband für Bayern,
1959), pp.11-23.

[4]J.D.C. Fisher, <u>Christian Initiation: The Reformation Period</u> (London:SPCK, 1970), pp.160-162.

[5]Maurer, op. cit., p.13.

[6]Fisher, <u>Christian Initiation: Baptism in the Medieval West,</u> pp.132-133.

[7]Ibid., p.134.

[8]Maurer, op. cit., p12.

[9]Paul K. Jewett, _Infant Baptism and the Covenant of Grace_ (Grand Rapids: Eerdmans, 1978), pp.18-19.

[10]Fisher, _Christian Initiation: Baptism in the Medieval West_, pp.104-105.

[11]Maurer, op. cit., p.14.

[12]Fisher, _Christian Initiation: Baptism in the Medieval West_, pp.127-130.

[13]Ibid., pp.131-132; Maurer, op. cit., p.15.

[14]Nathan D. Mitchell, "Dissolution of the Rite of Christian Initiation," in _Made, Not Born_, pp.66-67.

[15]Ibid., p.68. The idea was, however, not novel with Thomas, but is found already in John the Deacon at Rome about the end of the fifth century. See Lampe, op. cit., pp.302-303.

[16]Ibid., pp.68-69.

[17]Maurer, op. cit., p.16.

[18]Lampe, op. cit., pp.261-283; 297-305.

[19]Maurer, op. cit., pp.17; 39. Also J.D.C. Fisher, _Christian Initiation: The Reformation Period_ (London: SPCK, 1970), p.168.

[20]Maurer, op. cit., p.18.

[21]Kucharek, op.cit., p.153.

[22]See the article "Confirmation" by Piet Fransen in _Sacramentum Mundi: An Encyclopedia of Theology, Vol. 1_ (New York: Herder and Herder, 1968), p.408.

[23]Maurer, op. cit., p.18.

[24]Ibid.

[25]Roland H. Bainton, _Erasmus of Christendom_ (London: Collins, 1970), p.329.

[26]Ibid., pp.313-314.

^{27}Maurer, op. cit., pp.20-21; also Alois Stenzel, S.J., "Temporal and Supra-Temporal in the History of the Catechumenate and Baptism" in <u>Concilium/Vol.22</u> (New York: Paulist Press, 1967), pp.38-39.

^{28}Maurer, op. cit., p.21.

^{29}Ibid., pp.21-22.

Chapter Four

CONFIRMATION IN THE SIXTEENTH CENTURY REFORMATION

The trajectory which the developing doctrine and practice of confirmation had followed since the close of the New Testament period had about run its course. If the trajectory which had been plotted was accurate, the High Middle Ages would have found the rite of confirmation, as it was then practiced, right on target. But if there was an early miscalculation in the plotting of that trajectory, by this time the development could have brought it far off its intended course. The gathering ferment of the Late Middle Ages, particularly insofar as it also touched upon confirmation, was a sure signal that something was not right. Several midcourse corrections had been attempted, with that of Erasmus, perhaps, holding out the greatest promise. But there was a growing sense that it was too little, too late, and a radical new beginning may have become necessary.

This was the situation facing the Roman Catholic monk, priest, and professor of theology, Martin Luther (1483-1546), and it is to the Reformation largely catalyzed by him to which we must now turn. Coming from his own profound experience of spiritual renewal through a new appropriation of God's unconditional grace in Jesus Christ as taught in the New Testament, Luther reset a trajectory for Christian teaching, believing, and living. This occurred by a mighty blast of what we might call his course-correcting, Reformation rocket - biblical theology fueled by the powerful gospel of justification by God's grace in Jesus Christ received through faith alone (Rom. 1:16-17; 5:1-11).In this Luther differed from many of the promotors of reform both before and after him. Some, like Erasmus, had sought reform by a polite thrust toward New Testament "simplicity," fueled not, however, with the divine gospel of justification but with the humanistic gospel of the imitation of Christ - a gospel which indeed was more of a plastic imitation than it was an incarnation of the genuine article. Others, like those whom their opponents disparagingly called Anabaptists, were bolder than Erasmus and literally did start over again with an individualized confession of faith, rebaptism, and a personal commitment to follow the Christ of the New Testament as literally as possible, all of which, of course, involved a more or less comprehensive rejection of ecclesiastical traditions not explicitly attested in the New Testament.

Luther's biblical theology, however, did not nec-
essitate such a superficially radical break with tradition. Since his theology was fueled not by literalis-
tic attempts to reproduce New Testament forms but rather by a radical new release of New Testament substance
in the dynamic of the gospel of justification, Luther
could initiate a reform movement within the church in
which he found himself without totally rejecting its
traditions and institutions and wishing to start all
over. However, history conspired against this reform
movement and turned it into the denominational confessionalism which we have inherited today and which is
representatively expressed in the history of the diversification of confirmation as we shall now attempt to
trace it.

I   Confirmation for Luther and his Followers

Luther was not a man to weigh his words before he
expressed himself; at least, not if by doing so would
risk losing the point of the truth he thought he had
to express. Erasmus appears more gentle, but appear-
ances can be deceiving. He was not blunt, smashing,
and abusive, but he was cutting and knew how gently to
release a searing shaft of irony into the heart of his
victim's ego. Consequently someone has said: "If one
is to be demolished, does it so much matter whether one
is bludgeoned with a club or punctured by a rapier?"[1]
We must keep this in mind as we note some of Luther's
untempered language relative to confirmation. We must
push past his language and discover the basis for the
ordinarily righteous indignation which moved him to
such frequently unfortunate intemperance of expression.

In perhaps his best known but least understood description of confirmation he colorfully calls it monkey business, fanciful deception, and mumbo-jumbo.[2]
Taken out of context this would suggest that Luther saw
nothing positive in it at all, but in its context this
critique is seen to be particularly levelled at a lega-
listic consequence of the sacramentalized understanding
of confirmation, namely, the stipulations of an evolved
and involved canon law forbidding marriage between people "related" through sponsorships at baptism and confirmation. Luther was convinced that a church which
had lost its bearings was using such artificial marriage impediments as money-making devices, and that
these mercenary schemes had been piously cloaked in the

appeal to certain falsely sacramentalized church rites.
If such mercenary "monkey business" was the result of
the sacramental emphasis in Medieval confirmation,
Luther wanted nothing to do with it.

But it is clear that Luther's rejection of sacramental confirmation went still deeper than the above
reaction to an obvious abuse. In his mind Medieval confirmation was falsified at its very root - at the point
of its relation to biblical theology and its gospel dynamic. In a major work from the year 1520, entitled
"The Babylonian Captivity of the Church," Luther under-
took an elaborate examination of the whole sacramental
system of the church, concentrating upon baptism and the
Lord's Supper, but touching also upon confirmation and
the other rites which involve a laying on of hands or
an anointing. Here he insists that confirmation cannot
be a sacrament in the strict sense, for Christ did not
command it as a rite to which he attached the promise
of salvation; and now to give it such significance
would make it a man-made competitor with the saving
means which Christ had established. He insisted, in
effect, on the distinction between what the New Testament prescribes and what it merely describes. And he
was sure that the New Testament did not even describe
anything that looked like rites which had come to be
called "Confirmation" and "Extreme Unction."

But Luther did appreciate the New Testament significance of a laying on of hands. He wrote: "Would that
there were in the church such a laying on of hands as
there was in apostolic times, whether we chose to call
it confirmation or healing. But there is nothing left
of it now . . . ." Yet later he adds: "There is no
doubt at all that, even if today such a prayer were made
over a sick man [Jas. 5:15; 1:6; Mk. 11:24; 16:18] ,
that is, made in full faith by older, graver, saintly
men, as many as we wished would be healed. For what
could not faith do?"[3] Here it would seem as though the
New Testament connection between confirmation and the
experience of charismata was once again struggling to
break through.[4]

A look at Luther's liturgical writings and reforms,
however, indicates that he initially had little appreciation for confirmation as a rite. Whereas he produced revised liturgies for Baptism, the Eucharist, Confession, Marriage, and Ordination, he has no comparable
"Rite of Confirmation."[5] This has prompted some inter-
preters to claim Luther's understanding of the repeatable laying on of hands in private absolution as the

genuine "confirmation" of the gift already given in
baptism.[6] Although Luther's reconstruction of confirmation may have begun with such a simplistic emphasis
on the centrality of justification, he did not insist
that it remain so narrowly understood, and for this
reason he could speak approvingly of Martin Bucer's
(1491-1551) contributions in this direction.[7] But before describing Bucer's confirmation rite in greater
detail, it would be well for us to get an overview of
the diversification of opinion on confirmation emerging
at this time.

It has been suggested that out of the tangled mass
of influences and counterinfluences at work in the sixteenth century, no less than six different major types
of confirmation are able to be discerned within the
Lutheran Church alone. These may be characterized as
catechetical, hierarchical, sacramental, traditional,
pietistic, and rationalistic, with the latter two not
really congealing until the 17th and 18th centuries
respectively.[8] Others have suggested a less systematic and a more historical division by simply asking
whether the form of confirmation practiced was more dependent upon Luther or upon Erasmus. Confirmation
types dependent upon Luther emphasized a remembrance
of one's baptismal grace as preparation for first communion, whereas Erasmian types emphasized a necessary
completion of baptism through the renewal of baptismal
vows and a psychologizing of the sacramental element
with no particular relation to first communion.[9] In
the following we shall use both approaches to sort out
what happened to confirmation on the Lutheran scene.

1) <u>The Catechetical Type</u>

We have already seen how Erasmus promoted a cate-
chetical-type confirmation climaxing in the renewal of
baptismal vows. The interest in catechetical instruction among Lutherans, however, developed with more of
an eye to preparation for first communion. Luther's
catechism functioned particularly as a basis for instruction and pastoral examination of those preparing
for participation in the Lord's Supper, especially if
this was a first participation. And the faith which
Luther insisted was needed in order to benefit from
the sacrament was a faith which could not be characterized merely as "knowledge," but which rather had to
come to a focus in "trust." When upon such examination
the pastor were to find the faith "good and sincere,"
Luther found no fault if the pastor then "lays hands

on them and confirms them."10 Luther seemed uncertain
whether such a practice should be necessarily repeated
at intervals or whether once in a lifetime might suf-
fice.11 He apparently felt that pastoral experience
would dictate the practice, since it was not a sacrament with a specific command from Christ.

This catechetical type of "confirmation," which
was essentially a private pastoral ministry and not a
formal religious rite with a public ceremony, was the
earliest Lutheran practice, but it soon had to give
equal place to another practice.

2) The Hierarchical Type

Insofar as Lutherans utilize a "Rite of Confirmation," such a rite usually has its roots in the "Hierarchical Type" developed by Martin Bucer, particularly
for Hesse in 1538/39. Bucer's earliest influence were
the humanist ideas of Erasmus, but these were later
modified by his contact with Luther. In fact, he is
said to have effected a type of synthesis between
Luther and Erasmus.12 Relative to confirmation this
meant that Bucer combined the pedagogical and ethical
concerns of Erasmus with the theological and pastoral
concerns of Luther, introducing a public vow wherein
the child pledged to surrender to Christ and to submit
to the discipline of the Christian congregation.
Though Luther had himself hesitated to formalize such
a discipline, he did approve of the attempt on Bucer's
part to do so.13 It is what he himself seems to have
had in mind in 1526 when he wrote of an "evangelical
order" for "those who want to be Christians in earnest"
but for which "I have not yet the people or persons."14

When Bucer put together this hierarchical (or dis-
ciplinary) type of confirmation, he was not merely com-
posing a theoretical synthesis of his mentors, Erasmus
and Luther, while he sat comfortably uninvolved in his
ivory tower, but he was rather trying to meet what he
considered legitimate concerns of Anabaptists who found
Lutheran congregations coping poorly with moral laxity.
To meet this need Bucer developed and formalized a dis-
ciplinary concept of confirmation without, however,
following the Anabaptists in their anti-sacramental
bias.15 We can see here the roots of the developing
dialectic between an understanding of church as "sacramental community" and as "intentional community."
Here baptism in its narrow sense establishes sacramental community and confirmation expresses its inten-

tional dimensions, while the Lord's Supper once again
reinforces both intentions in an irreversible dialectic running from "gift" to "task."

Open to misunderstanding was Bucer's reintroduc-
tion of the formula "Receive the Holy Spirit" in connection with the laying on of hands. Such a formula
could be interpreted to mean that something less than
that had happened at baptism. On the other hand it
could also mean, as it probably does in Acts 8:14-19,
that a particular <u>manifestation</u> of the Spirit's presence was now to be "received," though not his <u>person</u>,
which had already been received in baptism. But a discussion of this problem leads us to the next type of
confirmation.

3) The Sacramental Type

It was particularly Bucer and those under his influence - even as far away as Thomas Cranmer (1489-
1556) in England, whose "Book of Common Prayer" (1549
and 1552) was directly affected by Bucer's thought -
who are considered to have promoted a sacramental type
of confirmation. This element came to expression in
Bucer's retention of the laying on of hands as part of
a formal rite which expressed the reception of the Holy
Spirit. There is, however, a great deal of disagree-
ment as to the precise meaning of this rite for Bucer.
Luther himself had not rejected it as a "sacramental
ceremony," as long as it did not become a sacrament
necessary for salvation or a rite signifying anything
more than what is taught in 1 Tim. 4:4-5, namely,
"that any creature whatsoever may be consecrated by
the Word and by prayer."[17] What Luther could not abide
was anything which would reduce baptism to something
less than the womb of or for all sacramental grace that
it was.[18]

Interestingly enough it was not the fear of a
false sacramentalizing of the laying on of hands that
finally carried the day. Nevertheless, a certain hesi-
tancy has been a constant reminder of the caution which
must be exercised in order to avoid at this point an
over-interpretation of the laying on of hands and an
under-interpretation of baptism. Even Martin Chemnitz
(1522-86) and Jacob Andreae (1528-90), two key figures
in the development of Lutheran confessionalism, advocated its use in a confirmation rite, if it could be
done without superstition and without offense.[19] But
the emphasis was on the Spirit's activity in "streng-

thening" the confirmands through "the Word" in faithfulness to the confession which they had just made. The
rite did not betray any expectation of charismatic
manifestations such as were evidenced in the New Testament period.

4) The Traditional Type

By this type is meant one which comes as close as
possible to inherited Medieval practice without be-
traying Lutheran confessional principles. The classic
example of this is the Church Order for Mark-Branden-
burg of 1540.[20]   It was authored by several men who
were Lutheran in orientation but who had a particularly
deep appreciation for the received tradition. Although it emphasized catechetical instruction and examination, it did not call for a renewal of vows as did
Erasmus and Bucer, nor did it direct this instruction
toward first-communion as did Luther. It simply took
the Medieval practice and made it what it idealisti-
cally should have been, namely, ample instruction from
the pastor and regular and conscientious confirmation
through the bishop, who if he could not carry out his
duties was to delegate them to the pastor but under
the observation of one of his learned advisors and
assistants. Easter and Pentecost were designated as
the most appropriate occasions for carrying out confirmations, but this was not a binding restriction.
Confirmation occurred after episcopal examination dealing with the truths of the catechism, the confirmand's
ability to pray, and his or her understanding of Christian discipleship. Thereupon the bishop prayed God to
"confirm, preserve, and strengthen" them in the same
and laid his hands upon them, also making the sign of
the cross upon their foreheads. The use of chrism was
not enjoined, although it was retained in connection
with baptism. Yet even here it was emphasized that it
is the Holy Spirit who anoints us in baptism and makes
us Christians and not the chrism which is only a sign
of this.

Again it is important to note that even though
Luther himself had not produced a formal rite of confirmation, when he was asked to give his opinion regarding the above discussed church order, he joined
Melanchthon and Justus Jonas in giving it his approval.[21] But the omission in this church order of any
mention of an expectation of the manifestation of charismatic gifts continues to be glaring in the face of
the New Testament witness.

II Confirmation in Lutheran Confessional Theology

To complete our sketch of what was happening to confirmation during the first two generations of the Lutheran Reformation, we must still look at two important sources - the theology of Luther's closest co-reformer, Philip Melanchthon, and the theology of Lutheranism's confessional documents in The Book of Concord.[22]

Melanchthon (1497-1560) is known as an outstanding biblical humanist and the leading educator in the Lutheran Reformation. He received extraordinary praise from both Luther and Erasmus. In the first edition (1521) of his Loci communes he contends that "faith is confirmed by this [participation in the Lord's Table] sign," but he fails to see how the rites of the laying on of hands and of unction "have been given as signs to signify grace for a certainty."[23] He thus agrees with Luther's distinction between essential sacraments and helpful sacramentals and with the connection between confirmation and the Lord's Supper, although Melanchthon at this point says nothing about catechetical instruction as preparation for first communion. The 1535 edition of the Loci includes confirmation among the sacraments in the wider sense, but the Erasmian doctrinal examination and repetition of baptismal vows are now emphasized.[24] The Loci of 1541 base in the practice of the early church a proposal to combine catechetical examination, confession of faith, and prayer with the laying on of hands into one liturgical action.[25] By 1543 Melanchthon could cooperate with Bucer in compiling for the reform-minded Archbishop Hermann of Cologne a church order which promoted a confirmation altogether in the style of Bucer's work in Hesse.[26] Melanchthon and Bucer were coming to be of one mind about many things in theology, including what some have called their "unionistic" tendencies.

However, Melanchthon was not merely an individualistic Lutheran professor expressing his personal theological opinions, but certain of his writings carried such weight that they were included in that commonly accepted "canon" of Lutheran confessional writings which came to be known as The Book of Concord. It was published in 1580 but contained documents dating from 1529 to 1577, with writings from Luther and Melanchthon representing the seminal first generation of Lutheranism and the 1577 document called "The Formula of Concord" written basically by four second-generation

50

Lutherans.[27]

In _The Book of Concord_ we find no positive reference to a rite of confirmation such as we have seen was actually practiced in many of the Lutheran churches. As a rite it is referred to only twice, the first time as being unnecessary for salvation and the second time as being part of the "humbug" which bishops had used to enhance their own jurisdiction.[28] However, in a manner similar to his _Loci_ of 1521 Melanchthon uses the verbal form, "confirm," in a positive sense to refer not only to "external signs" such as baptism and the Lord's Supper, but also to "good works" which follow as a fruit of faith (charismata), all of which function to "_confirm_ terrified minds to believe more firmly that their sins are forgiven."[29] Here Melanchthon allows "good works" as the "fruit of the Spirit," that is, charismatic manifestations in the broad sense, to function as a means whereby "confirmation" occurs.

Luther himself had done something similar in his Large Catechism when in his explanation of the fifth petition of the Lord's Prayer he understands the clause "as we forgive our debtors" as a "condition" and "sign" which serves to "strengthen and gladden our conscience."[30] Here also a "fruit of the Spirit," namely, the extension of forgiveness to our neighbor, stands as a charismatic manifestation serving to "confirm" our own faith in the Good News of God's forgiveness.

Again in his Large Catechism, as he discusses "Baptism," Luther discovers "confirmation" in the "wonders from heaven" which were manifested at the occasion of Jesus' baptism.[31] Without expanding upon this idea Luther is here bringing the notion of confirmation and the charismata into juxtaposition.

Finally, in the "Formula of Concord" Melanchthon's use of 2 Pet.1:10 in his "Apology" is quoted approvingly as an example of how the "fruit of the Spirit" serve to "_confirm_ your call."[32] The Lutheran Confessions quite consistently, then, avoid focusing upon a rite of confirmation and instead relate the notion of confirmation to the on-going manifestation of charismata. The closest thing to an approved _rite_ of confirmation to be found in the Lutheran Confessions would be an expression of the catechetical type, namely, the requirement that pastors and ministers "instruct and examine the youth publicly," thus demanding a process of catechization in preparation for participation in the Lord' Supper.[33] But nothing is said here regarding a ceremonial

repetition of baptismal vows or a blessing prayed down
through the laying on of hands. The latter is called
a "sacrament" only insofar as it is interpreted as an
expression of the command given to the church to ap-
point ministers of the Word.[34] It imparts no "character" but expresses rather a "call."

Accordingly the Lutheran Confessions do not de-
mand a confirmation rite which should serve as the completion of an otherwise deficient baptism. They do,
however, understand the sanctifying exercise of baptismal faith as that which in an on-going way works
at the completion of that which God has already begun
and continues in baptism.[35] For its completion baptism requires no additional sacrament such as confirmation, but it does indeed require daily acts of faith
which will allow God to grant an experiential confirmation to that faith again and again until the ultimate confirmation occurs in the resurrection on the
last day.[36]

III   Confirmation in the Reformed and Anabaptist Traditions

Ulrich Zwingli (1484-1531), the initiator of the
Reformation in Switzerland, maintained that he was not
dependent upon Martin Luther, but that he had begun to
preach the Gospel of Christ in the year 1516 "before
any man in our region had so much as heard the name
Luther."[37] Of all the reformers (including Melanchthon)
Zwingli was the most strongly influenced by the humanism espoused by Erasmus, although his theology of reform developed beyond that of the prince of the Human-
ists. For instance, in 1523 Zwingli utterly rejected
the medieval sacrament of confirmation but proposed
in its stead an orderly form of religious instruction
for the youth and a public renewal of the baptismal
covenant. Thus in the negative aspect of his reform
he followed Luther, but in the positive he followed
Erasmus.[38] For Zwingli, confirmation was not an action on God's part or on the part of the church, but
an act on the part of the catechumen who by his public
confession "confirmed" his faith and put his baptism
into effect.

Such a confirmation of faith appealed to some of
Zwingli's compatriots like Konrad Grebel (c.1498-1526)
and Felix Manz (c.1500-27), but they went further than
Zwingli and insisted that the appropriate rite to accompany such a "faith confession" was baptism itself,

and they introduced rebaptism, or better, adult believer's baptism, as the fitting replacement for infant
baptism with its subsequent confirmation. Though Zwingli adamantly continued to insist upon infant baptism,
with some degree of melancholy he admitted of the Anabaptists that "they have sprung from us."39 Like Erasmus, who also repudiated the consequences drawn by the
Anabaptists, Zwingli's position on confirmation lent itself handily as a theological rationale for the adult
believer's baptism practiced by the Anabaptists. As
one commentator has put it: "He decided to walk with
the Fathers and contrary to the Anabaptists in retain-
ing the usage of infant baptism, but at the same time
to walk with the Anabaptists and contrary to the Fathers
by denying the necessity of infant baptism."40

It is difficult to know whether to identify Thomas
Cranmer (1489-1556) with the Reformation of Luther or
with that of Calvin. His own work has been described
as "more of a developing process than the fulfillment
of a set plan."41 In sequence his reforming tendencies
seemed to look like those of Erasmus, Luther, Melanchthon, Bucer, and Calvin, although he always also seemed
to carry considerable from each previous phase with him.
His place in church history is secured by his liturgical
and doctrinal formulations as these were expressed in
the two editions of the "Book of Common Prayer" (1549/
52) and in the "Forty-Two Articles" (1549/52). He held
firmly to the sacramental understanding of baptism but
contemporary Anglican scholars are not agreed whether
his understanding of confirmation was a valid continuation of the medieval sacrament of confirmation (con-
ceived particularly as a solemn intercessory act by the
bishop, effectively working "an increase of grace") or
whether Cranmer's reform "irretrievably weakened" the
case for the indispensability of sacramental confirma-
tion.42 Here, as so often, Cranmer, and the Anglican
Reformation which he fathered, is not easily pigeon-
holed but continues to express a reformation in process
and open to a variety of interpretations.43

John Calvin (1509-1564) and Geneva are almost syn-
onyms, having been made that by Calvin's arduous reformation activity in that city. Zwingli's premature death
on the battlefield had left something of a vacuum of
leadership in the Swiss Reformation, a vacuum which Calvin filled with great reluctance but also with great
success. His mind which had been carefully honed on a
lawyer's education was also deeply influenced by humanism and by Lutheranism. The sharply nuanced remarks
which he makes on the question of "Confirmation" in the

final Latin edition (1559) of his <u>Institutes of the
Christian Religion</u> demonstrate vividly all three influences. The following is a summary of those remarks:

1) The early church required that children, who had
   been baptized as infants and who had therefore
   not been subjected to the prebaptismal catechumenate, be subjected to it after baptism upon
   reaching adolescence. Parents were to present
   such children to the bishop for examination and
   confession of their faith. The bishop would
   upon approval of their faith dismiss them with
   the laying on of hands (understood as a solemn
   blessing).

2) A later age transformed this practice into "a
   kind of fictitious confirmation as a divine
   sacrament." But since the rite has no command
   of God, its practice becomes "sacrilegious aud-
   acity."

3) The attempt to base confirmation as a sacrament
   on the practice of the apostles is misdirected.
   What the apostles did at Samaria, for instance
   (Acts 8:15-17), was to lay on their hands and
   thereby actually "dispense" the "visible gifts
   of the Spirit." "But these miraculous powers
   and manifest operations, which were distributed
   by the laying on of hands, have ceased." The
   bishops cannot imitate what the apostles effected through the laying on of hands.

4) It is "nefarious" to claim that baptism cannot
   be "duly completed without confirmation." Episcopal confirmation "is a noted insult to baptism, the use of which it obscures - nay, abo-
   lishes."

5) Confirmation in the true sense and "without in-
   jury to baptism" would be catechetical in nature. After such instruction "a boy of ten
   years of age would present himself to the
   Church, to make a profession of faith, would be
   questioned on each head, and give answers to
   each. If he was ignorant of any point, or did
   not well understand it, he would be taught.
   Thus, while the whole Church looked on and wit-
   nessed, he would profess the one true sincere
   faith with which the body of the faithful, with
   one accord, worship one God."[44]

More sharply than any whom we have studied up to this point, Calvin distinguishes between what we might call "apostolic confirmation" and "ecclesiastical confirmation." The former must, according to Calvin, be strictly limited to the age of the apostolic church. Only during this severely limited period did God grant sacramental power to the laying on of hands in the sense that visible and miraculous gifts of the Spirit were thereby actually "dispensed." Thereafter this gesture could be defined only as St. Augustine did, namely, as "prayer over the man."[45] When the Medieval church, however, tried to transform this ecclesiastical _blessing_ into an episcopal _sacrament_ necessary to complete baptism, it improperly, to say the least, attempted to imitate what was given only to the apostolic church.

But we must ask whether Calvin's critique of the medieval theology of confirmation has not been too cheaply bought. If the church today is to be truly apostolic, why should apostolic confirmation cease? Granted that "episcopal confirmation" was a questionable imitation of apostolic practice, why did no one really stop to review the biblical evidence rather than merely to make dispensationalist assumptions, reflecting a humanist's view of a "golden age" of the church, that the charismatic manifestations were no longer to be expected?[46] The Medieval solution had at least kept alive the memory of a _God_ who confirms. Meanwhile the Anabaptist solution, although it retained an expression of the biblical experiential dimension of confirmation, seemed to invert the biblical order of "promised salvation, faith, experience" into "experience, faith, promised salvation."[47] What God had joined together according to his plan, the churches were still separating or joining together according to their plan. But would they have been able to hear God's plan more clearly if they had attentively listened to each other while also reading their Bibles?

IV Confirmation in Roman Catholic Reformation
    Theology

The Diet of Augsburg of 1530 with its influential "Augsburg Confession" was not the only attempt in the sixteenth century to heal the festering wound in the torn and broken body of Christ caused by the inability of the contending theological parties to be reconciled. Even after the Lutheran movement congealed into a confessional denomination, to be followed soon by others, attempts at reconciliation continued to be made until the canons of the Council of Trent (1545-63) appeared to make all future attempts futile. For our overview of the historical development of the doctrine and practice of confirmation in the sixteenth century we must look briefly yet at the Colloquy of Regensburg (1541/46), the Augsburg and Leipzig Interims (1548), the Council of Trent, and an extended response to it by the Lutheran theologian, Martin Chemnitz (1522-1586).

The Diet of Regensburg in 1541 has been said to be the high-water mark of Protestant-Catholic dialogue in the sixteenth century.[48] The key figures were the reform-minded John Gropper and Caspar Contarini for the Roman Catholics and the reconciliation-minded Bucer, Melanchthon, and Calvin for the Reformers. A document which had been worked out in advance by Gropper and Bucer in private conference, the now-famous Regensburg Book, was the agreed upon basis for the colloquy. Crucial was the union formula on justification, which, however, both Luther and Rome ultimately found unacceptable. But of interest is also the debate which ensued around the question of confirmation.[49]

The theses of the Regensburg Book on confirmation were by and large bound to the traditional medieval understanding of the sacrament, but Bucer attempted to push the idea of its relation to a disciplined practice of the Lord's Supper into the foreground of the discussion. Yet by emphasizing the formation of conscience through careful catechetical instruction, he was appealing to the Erasmian inclinations found in men like Gropper and Contarini.[50] Unfortunately, the end result of the Diet of Regensburg was that, at the instance of the emperor, it was decided that the prelates should simply work along traditional lines at reforming church conditions and administration in their jurisdiction.[51]

Though the Regensburg Colloquy might be termed an attempt at reconciliation, the Augsburg and Leipzig Interims (1548) were really more in the nature of compromises, with Luther's outspoken voice having been silenced by death and the Council of Trent having begun to rally and to strengthen the Roman Catholic Counter-Reformation. The Augsburg Interim represented theologically the Roman position; and though the Leipzig Interim presented a more reformed doctrine of justification and good works, it nevertheless retained many Roman usages and continued to require the recognition of the seven sacraments of Roman Catholicism.

For years the Reformers had been challenging Rome
to summon a "free council," that is, one in which the
"protesting" parties would not be treated as defendants
but in which they together with other unpartisan men
could discuss and decide the schismatic questions according to the Word of God alone.[52] A look at the
three canons of the Council of Trent on confirmation
betrays the reason why the Reformers were reluctant to
attend or to expect much from the council. They read
as follows:

> Can. 1. If anyone says that the confirmation
> of those baptized is an empty ceremony and not
> a true and proper sacrament; or that of old it
> was nothing more than a sort of instruction,
> whereby those approaching adolescence gave an
> account of their faith to the Church, let him
> be anathema.
>
> Can. 2. If anyone says that those who ascribe
> any power to the holy chrism of confirmation,
> offers insults to the Holy Ghost, let him be
> anathema.
>
> Can. 3. If anyone says that the ordinary mini-
> ster of holy confirmation is not the bishop a-
> lone, but any simple priest, let him be anathema.[53]

An assessment of the Council of Trent by a Roman
Catholic historian says that "Trent gave every indica-
tion of defending to the hilt whatever was attacked by
the Protestants or ridiculed by the Catholic reformers."[54] It simply left little room for dialogue, but
such as it did was taken up by Martin Chemnitz, known
especially for his important contribution to the formulation of the Lutheran _Formula of Concord_ (1577),[55]
but also for his massive _Examination of the Council of
Trent_ (1565-1573). Chemnitz was spurred into publishing this research by the attack made upon him by one of
the council fathers, the traditionalist James Payva
d'Andrada (1528-1576?). A summary of his thirty-four
page (in our edition)[56] response to the three canons
on confirmation quoted above now follows:

> 1) The principal point of the controversy is the
>   constant antithesis between baptism and con-
>   firmation, so that "whatever effects are as-
>   cribed to confirmation are by that very fact
>   denied or taken away from baptism."[57]

2) The Holy Spirit works efficaciously in believers, not without means, but through certain
means or instruments divinely instituted for
this purpose. Scripture does not record the
institution of a sacrament of confirmation
through anointing with oil or the laying on
of hands, but rather witnesses to the following "means" for preserving and strengthening
the grace conferred in baptism; the Word, the
Eucharist, faith, prayer, afflictions, and the
exercise of the mental gifts we have received.[58]

3) It is incumbent upon the papalists to demonstrate or show a command of God, that what the
apostles did (Acts 8:14-17; 19:6) is to be imitated, employed, and frequently resorted to in
the church until the end of the age, until
Christ comes in judgment.[59] /In this context
it is interesting to note that Chemnitz never
explicitly alludes to Lk. 11:13._/

4) The apostles had both a command and a promise
for what they did. If the outpouring of the
perceptible gifts still perdured in the church,
also the imposition of hands would rightly be
employed, which customarily was used also in
connection with prayers, and chiefly when miracles were performed through the hands of apostles (Acts 5:12). But it is beyond controversy
that these miracles have long ceased in the
church. Therefore what is written concerning
the apostles (Acts 1:4-8; 8:14-17; 19:5-6) was
temporary, not universal nor for all time.[60]
/Interestingly, the cessation of charismatic
manifestations is demonstrated by Chemnitz not
through biblical reference but through empirical
observation and logically drawn conclusions.
How does this comport with Luther's openness to
charismatic manifestations as noted in the text
to footnote 4 above?_/

5) The ancient church does not support the papalist
division between baptism and confirmation. Where
such is indicated, it is under heretical Montan-
ist influence.[61]

6) Even Cyril of Jerusalem (c.315-386) cannot be
made to support the claim, since he speaks of
oil merely as the symbol of the Holy Spirit
which is, however, efficaciously given

through the water of baptism.[62] His insistence
that we must nevertheless be anointed with this
symbol is erroneous.[63]

7) The papalists have confused the meaning of the
biblical imposition of hands with an anointing
with oil which in the ancient church had a dis-
tinctly different meaning.[64]

8) Formerly the action of baptism was one, in the
sense of being continuous and conjoined, with
anointing and the imposition of hands. The
historical reasons for the separation into
distinct sacraments are as follows:

   a) The bishop laid hands on converted heretics.
   They were not rebaptized but were rather recognized through this gesture of love.

   b) The bishop anointed or laid hands on such
   as were irregularly baptized in emergency
   situations. He thereby approved and confirmed the validity of the baptism already
   received.

   c) The bishop would lay hands on those who had
   been baptized in his absence by presbyters
   and deacons. He did this out of his shep-
   herding instinct for manifesting the purity
   and the unity of the church. Unfortunately
   this custom began to be interpreted as a
   sacramental necessity.[65]

9) The rite of confirmation can be used in a godly
fashion and for the edification of the church
in the following way:

   a) After catechetical instruction a child baptized in infancy should be admonished to
   remember his or her baptism - its covenantal
   nature, its renunciation of Satan, and its
   promise of obedience.

   b) The child should give his or her own public
   profession of this doctrine and faith.

   c) He or she should be thoroughly examined in
   all the chief parts of the Christian religion.

d) He or she should recognize how this confession sets one apart from all that opposes and disagrees with it.

e) He or she should be seriously exhorted to persevere in this baptismal covenant and confession.

f) Public prayer, to which the laying on of hands could be added, should be made for the confirmed that God would deign, by his Holy Spirit, to govern, preserve, and strengthen him or her in this confession.[66]

10) The papalists err in rejecting such a confirmation. They reject it because they want it to be a sacrament functioning _ex opere operato_. They thereby prefer to enhance the questionable status of bishops rather than to maintain the Scriptural validity of baptism.[67]

This lengthy summary of Chemnitz's response to the canons of Trent on confirmation seeks to teach us as much about the Roman Catholic Reformation's understanding of confirmation as it teaches us about the Reformation for which Chemnitz was arguing. But perhaps that was the problem. We have become privy to a theological _debate_ about confirmation rather than a genuine _dialogue_. The diversification of opinions about confirmation during the sixteenth century Reformation became entrenched in confessional positions with little capacity for listening to differing points of view. And as we shall see in the following chapter, things will get worse before they get better.

Footnotes

[1]Bainton, op. cit., p.336.

[2]Arthur C. Repp, _Confirmation in the Lutheran Church_ (St. Louis: Concordia, 1964), pp.15-16; LW 45: 8, 24.

[3]LW 36: 91f., 121.

[4]Three recent Luther studies document this struggling tendency in the Reformation, namely: John Warwick Montgomery, _Principalities and Powers_ (Minneapolis:

Bethany Fellowship, 1973), pp.180-187; Bengt R. Hoffman, _Luther and the Mystics_ (Minneapolis: Augsburg, 1976), pp.193-201; Karlfried Froelich, "Charismatic Manifestations and the Lutheran Incarnational Stance," in _The Holy Spirit in the Life of the Church_, ed. Paul D. Opsahl (Minneapolis: Augsburg, 1978), pp.136-157.

[5]LW 53 (Liturgy and Hymns).

[6]Maurer, op. cit., pp.24-25.

[7]In a letter to Anton Lauterbach (dec.1560) in Pirna Luther wrote: "The Hessian model of church discipline pleases me and if you should be able to establish something similar, you would be doing very well." (WA, Br 10, 284, 17ff.)

[8]Repp, op. cit., p.21.

[9]Maurer, op. cit., pp.19f.; 25; 37.

[10]Repp, op. cit., p.17; Maurer, op. cit., p.24.

[11]LW 53: 32f.

[12]Maurer, op. cit., p.28.

[13]See footnote seven, above, and Maurer, op. cit., p.30.

[14]LW 53: 63f.

[15]Repp., op. cit., p.29f.

[16]J.D.C. Fisher, _Christian Initiation: The Reformation Period_, pp.180-181.

[17]LW 36: 82, 122.

[18]LW 36: 59 - ". . . baptism is the first sacrament and the foundation of all the others without which none of the others can be received."

[19]Repp, op. cit., pp.41-43.

[20]J.D.C. Fisher, _Christian Initiation: The Reformation Period_, pp.182-184.

[21]Luther D. Reed, _The Lutheran Liturgy_ (Philadelphia: Fortress, 1947), pp.98-101.

[22]We will be citing from the edition by Theodore G. Tappert (Philadelphia: Fortress, 1959).

[23]Charles L. Hill, trans., _The Loci Communes of Philip Melanchthon_ (Boston: Meador, 1944), pp.258-259; Maurer, op. cit., p.33.

[24]Maurer, op. cit., p.33.

[25]Ibid.

[26]J.D.C. Fisher, _Christian Initiation: The Reformation Period_, pp.54-69; 194-203; Reed, op. cit., pp.102-105.

[27]See the historical introductions in Tappert, _The Book of Concord_.

[28]Ibid., pp.212.6; 332.73.

[29]Ibid., p.148.275-276.

[30]Ibid., p.433.93-98.

[31]Ibid., pp.439.21; 443.50.

[32]Ibid., pp.228.12-13; 556.33.

[33]Ibid., p.220.40-41; also p.56.6; 61.1; 312.1.

[34]Ibid., p.212.11-12.

[35]Ibid., pp.444-445.64-73.

[36]Ibid., pp.626-628.71-74.

[37]Bard Thompson, "Ulrich Zwingli," in B.A. Gerrish, ed., _Reformers in Profile_ (Philadelphia: Fortress, 1967), p.120.

[38]Maurer, op. cit., p.27.

[39]Jean Rilliet, _Zwingli: Third Man of the Reformation_, tr. Harold Knight (Philadelphia: Westminster, 1959 and 1964), p.139.

[40]Jewett, op. cit., pp.13-14; 78; 80.

[41]B.A. Gerrish, ed., _Reformers in Profile_ (Philadelphia: Fortress, 1967), pp.181-182.

[42] Charles U. Harris, "The Anglican Understanding of Confirmation," in Confirmation: History, Doctrine, and Practice, Kendig Brubaker Cully, ed. (Greenwich: Seabury, 1962), pp.21-25.

[43] Gerrish, op. cit., pp.178-182; J.D.C. Fisher, Christian Initiation: The Reformation Period, pp.89-95; 106-111; 236-243; 251-253.

[44] John Calvin, Institutes of the Christian Religion, Vol. II, tr. Henry Beveridge (Grand Rapids: Eerdmans, 1957), pp.625-632; also J.D.C. Fisher, Christian Initiation: The Reformation Period, pp.254-260.

[45] Calvin, op. cit., pp.631-632.

[46] Maurer, op. cit., pp.26; 33f.

[47] Leonel L. Mitchell, "Christian Initiation: The Reformation Period," in Made Not Born, pp.93-97; also Regin Prenter, Spiritus Creator (Philadelphia: Muhlenberg/Fortress, 1953), pp.247-254.

[48] John P. Dolan, History of the Reformation: A Conciliatory Assessment of Opposite Views (New York: Desclee, 1965), p.383.

[49] For these details see Robert Stupperich, Melanchthon, tr. Robert H. Fischer (Philadelphia: Westminster, 1955), pp.116-118; Maurer, op. cit., pp.31-32.

[50] Dolan, op. cit., pp.358; 383f.; 390.

[51] G.J. Van de Poll, Martin Bucer's Liturgical Ideas (Assen: Van Gorcum, 1954), pp.133-134.

[52] Stupperich, op. cit., pp.107; 109; 122; Dolan, op. cit., pp.400-401.

[53] Canons and Decrees of the Council of Trent. Original Texts with English Translation, tr. Rev. H.J. Schroeder, O.P. (St. Louis: Herder, 1941), pp.54-55.

[54] Dolan, op. cit., p.402.

[55] The Book of Concord, Tappert Edition, pp.463-636.

[56] Martin Chemnitz, Examination of the Council of Trent, Part II, tr. Fred Kramer (St. Louis: Concordia, 1978), pp.181-215.

[57]Ibid., pp.182-186; 196-197.

[58]Ibid., pp.188; 195.

[59]Ibid., pp.191-192; 194.

[60]Ibid., pp.191; 195.

[61]Ibid., pp.198-201.

[62]Ibid., pp.202-204.

[63]Ibid., pp.204-205.

[64]Ibid., pp.205-208.

[65]Ibid., pp.208-211.

[66]Ibid., p.212.

[67]Ibid., pp.213-215.

Chapter Five

CONFIRMATION: POST-REFORMATION UP TO THE PRESENT ERA

The varying and sometimes conflicting confessional positions which emerged out of the sixteenth century Reformation on the question of the doctrine and practice of confirmation had one merit. Even though the differences contributed to the disunity of the visible church, at no time in the previous history of the church had there been a more intense wrestling with the question. Earlier interpretations, which often did seem to stand in conflict with one another but which were able to be harmonized by depending upon their ambiguities, were during this period clarified to the point that with the ambiguities removed the conflicts became painfilly visible. Perhaps it is difficult to see the merit of that. But since a unity dependent upon ambiguities finally ends up frustrating good pastoral care, which can be good only when it is also based in truth, we will have to agree that the confessional conflicts of the sixteenth century had this merit that they were a struggle to discover the truth about confirmation.

And yet these struggles for truth left a lot to be desired, particularly since they were often carried on without sufficient expression of that kind of love which could have enabled the discovery of what was possibly a legitimate concern but which was unfortunately hidden beneath an opponent's polemically pointed arguments. Did the fathers at Trent really give the legitimate concerns of the Reformers a hearing and did they give them credit for anything else than the desire to foment division in the church? On the other hand, how much by this time did Reformers like Chemnitz and others want to hear the concerns of those fathers not merely with their minds, but also with their hearts? The context of Phil.2:5 would indicate that having the "mind" of Christ also involves having his "heart." The road to Jerusalem was never merely a "head-trip," but confessional polemics have often reduced the "gospel," which was being so boldly defended, to little more than that.

As we continue our historical sketch of confirmation throughout the Christian centuries and direct our attention now to the post-Reformation period up to the present era, we will concentrate our discussion upon the pendulum which was swinging back and forth between

the head and the heart - between concern for confirmation as a heady intellectual expression of the faith
and confirmation as a decisional expression of the
heart or even as an emotional expression of the soul.

I   Confirmation after Ignatius of Loyola

     Although Ignatius of Loyola (1491-1556) has not left
us either an explicit doctrine or practice of confirmation which in any way deviated from that expressed in
the canons and catechism of Trent, yet since his Spiritual Exercises and the Constitutions of the Society of
Jesus have left us with a method of spiritual formation
which has served as an important stimulus in the realm
of catechetical development, we will briefly consider
his contribution in this area.[1]

     It has been noted that despite their differences,
the ideals for reforming church and society as held by
Ignatius coincided closely with the aspirations of Erasmus as expressed in his Praise of Folly.[2] Both emphasized the need for such as would be willing to be soldiers of Christ, although Erasmus tended to universalize
that concept, making it applicable to all Christians,
whereas Ignatius seemed to limit it to those willing to
engage in the rigors of the Society of Jesus.[3] Yet, if
we think of the latter merely as such as took upon themselves the responsibility for evangelization and initiation into the Christian life and that in some essential
way all Christians should be willing to submit to such
"spiritual exercises," then Ignatius also had in mind
a program which would affect Christian society as a
whole.

     The Spiritual Exercises proposed by Ignatius suggest
that he had a grasp on the need for personal spiritual
experience in the life of the Christian. His approach
to reformation in the church was not one that affected
its hierarchical structures, but one which looked rather for a method of "reforming" the individual's heart,
enabling him to be loosed from an attachment to created
things by becoming instead utterly attached to the Creator.[4] Like Erasmus, then, he did not seek to undermine
the sacramental system of the church but to introduce
a method, not to say technique, for exploiting its
"givens" to the fullest. He never would contest those
givens. He simply concentrated his attention upon ways
and means for personally experiencing what supposedly
could have been objectively given at another place and

time, being willing enough to accept what the church
had traditionally taught about that.

Ignatius made claim to spiritual experiences
enough - experiences designated as "consolations" and
"illuminations," which came to expression by way of
dreams and visions, tears and raptures, and all of
which were embedded in the charism of the discernment
of spirits.[5] His mention of "vocal prayer, pronounced
slowly, rhythmically" has even reminded some of glossolalia.[6] Yet the way to such experience followed the
patterns suggested by earlier Spanish and German my-
stics - the way of progressive self-abnegation, the
way of psychological introspection and self-examination
encouraged by a rigorous asceticism.[7] It was a skewing
of the emphasis given in Acts 1:4 from a faith-full
waiting for the _promise_ to a particularly ascetic _wait-_
ing for the promise.

Although Ignatius' goal was _God_, his method emphasized _man_, an emphasis later to be criticized not only
by Protestant protagonists of God's grace, but also by
the Augustinian Catholic, Blaise Pascal (1623-62).[8] His
emphasis on the three traditional vows of poverty,
chastity, and obedience, but in addition on the more
confessionalistic fourth vow of obedience and service
to the Roman pontiff, understandably provoked reaction
in the Protestant camp where, as we shall see, there
developed a progressively narrow emphasis on a confirmation vow which pledged the confirmand among other
things to specific and continuing denominational, and
even congregational, loyalties.[9]

In Ignatius Loyola we find the pendulum which had
begun to swing between the mind and the heart at a sort
of midpoint. He knew and wished to emphasize the importance of each, but that by which both his mind and
his heart were fascinated was _man's obedient response_
to the grace of God rather than _God's gracious conde-_
scension to the need of man. And it would be some time
yet before confessional polemics could respond to the
critical question of the relationship between God's
grace and man's responsibility in any other way than
by a swing of the pendulum.

II Confirmation after English Puritanism

It has been suggested that in the churches of the
West the ritual structures of initiation can be reduced
essentially to three patterns - the two-stage (Roman

Catholics and Protestants who practice infant baptism
and a "confirmation" somewhat later); the one-stage
(Baptists who reject infant baptism but whose "believer's baptism" attempts to unite in one ritual act what
the paedobaptists had apparently separated into two); and
the no-stage (the Society of Friends and others who
reject sacraments altogether and apart from any ritual
emphasize an inward spirituality which expresses itself
in Christlikeness).[10] Related to these stereotypes we
find variations such as that proposed by English Puritanism.

Puritanism was a movement in the Church of England
during the reign of Elizabeth I (1558-1603) and the
first two Stuarts (James I, 1603-25; Charles I, 1625-
49). Even though the reign of all three represented a
gradual protestantizing of the Church of England, this
Anglican Church nevertheless remained far too "Catholic"
for the religious tastes of many, and among these were
the so-called "Puritans," who wished to "purify" the
Church from what they considered vestiges of Roman
Catholicism. Amongst these vestiges was "Confirmation,"
which the Puritans (especially Oliver Cromwell, 1599-
1658), along with Scotch Presbyterians (John Knox, 1505-
72; the Westminster Confession and the Westminster Cate-
chisms, 1643-47), criticized sharply. They considered
it a pseudo-sacrament and a derogation of the two domi-
nical sacraments. In their judgment baptism marked the
commencement of the Christian life and the Lord's Supper added "the seal of confirmation of that grace," a
notion which had already been advocated by Melanchthon
in the first edition of his Loci (1521).

In place of "Confirmation" the Puritans used a ceremony of admission to church membership, basing this rite
on acceptance of a "covenant," which was a solemn promise of fidelity to Christ and to the local congregation rather than a mere statement of belief. Puritans
continued to baptize their children, recalling the promise that the covenant was "to you and to your children," but church membership was more and more made conditional upon evidence of saving faith. Each person
had to look within himself for the "signs of election."
When the necessary signs of the work of God were manifest, an unbeliever could be brought into the church,
or a child could "own the covenant."

It has been noted that these features of Puritanism
indicated a respect for inward experience and a tendency toward self-analysis.[11] For all their differences
there was something in the air which here linked Puri-

tanism with some of the concerns of Ignatius Loyola as noted above. Cromwell's "New Model Army," - which consisted of zealous soldiers of various shades of Protestant belief, but who were infused with his own biblical faith, Puritanical simplicity, and a strong sense of divine mission - surpassed even Ignatius' spiritual "storm troopers" in violence of method relative to the implementation of reform. Here confirmation certainly did become an experience rather than a rite, and a matter of the heart rather than of the head, but one wonders whether the gift of implementing faith with the sword was really a charism given by the Holy Spirit for the confirmation of the faithful. Yet for all that, the Puritan program grew out of an earnest desire to understand precisely the will of God and to experience consciously his saving grace. At its best it was characterized by preaching, "prophesyings" (that is, meetings to discuss Scripture passages), catechizing, Bible readings, and family devotions. Also, the challenge and the space which "New England" afforded was able to channel its "violence" (Matt.11:12) in more constructive directions.[12] But confirmation as a ritualistic and sacramental act had in the Puritan tradition been cut off root and branch.

III   Confirmation after German Pietism

While Roman Catholicism, through the efforts of reformers like Ignatius Loyola, and Anglicanism, through the Puritan protest, were developing a religion of the heart, German Lutheranism continued to advance along the lines of a doctrinal orthodoxy which was developing a heady scholasticism all its own. The catechetical aspect of confirmation was emphasized, concentration being placed upon rote learning and convoluted theological expositions. The Roman Catholic Counter-Reformation was making effective inroads upon Lutheran territories and consequently confirmation vows in affected areas began to take on a polemical cast - as, for example, in the solemn promise to remain ever faithful to the Lutheran Church.[13] Simultaneously the recognition began to dawn that the battle could not be won simply at the level of the head, but the heart had to be captured if all was not to be once again lost. Thus the so-called "Pietist" movement arose with its design "to bring the head into the heart."

The precipitating event in the birth of German Pietism was the publication in 1675 of Philip Jacob Spener's (1635-1705) _Pia Desideria_. Here Spener set

forth his "devout wishes" for a reformation in the
Lutheran Church and beyond. He emphasized above all
the need for ministers who were themselves deeply converted and he pleaded for a general increase in devotional life. An apocalyptic note was introduced when
he linked the realization of his ideals to the conversion of the Jews and the fall of papal Rome. And like
Erasmus before him he hoped that the rite of confirmation could be harnessed in the service of such church
renewal. Thus confirmation was to concentrate on
reaching the individual's heart in order to effect his
or her conversion.[14]

Ignatius Loyola had formed the "Society of Jesus"
through the utilization of his Spiritual Exercises;
Oliver Cromwell had through his own charismatic leadership inspired a "New Model Army;" and now Spener hoped
by his reform of confirmation practices to bring into
being ecclesiolae, that is, groups of "converted" persons within the church, whose spiritually warming influence would thaw into renewal enlarging circles within congregations otherwise frozen into inactivity by a
moribund orthodoxy. Spener thought of baptism primarily
in covenant terms and therefore as something which, following Old Testament Deuteronomic precedent, needed to
be renewed regularly.[15] This thought he applied to confirmation, and accordingly he gave the vow, which Bucer
had earlier proposed as an integral part of the confirmation rite, a new meaning. Instead of speaking in this
context about "remembering" the baptismal covenant, he
emphasized a "renewal" of the covenant.[16] The change
may at first glance seem insignificant, but it allowed
in fact for an important shift in emphasis from the re-
appropriation of objectively given sacramental grace
to the subjective affirmation and reaffirmation of the
confirmand's commitment to Christ and his locally manifested body (ecclesiola).

Although Spener's emphasis on the development of
"Collegia Pietatis" (devotional house meetings) pre-
vented his subjective emphasis from working itself out
in an anti-church individualism, it did dramatically
raise the question regarding the relationship between
sacramental community and intentional community. He
came under much attack from the "Lutheran Orthodoxy"
by which he was surrounded, but actually he had no intention of undermining that orthodox doctrinal struc-
ture but only of providing a method whereby the life
which had grown cold within could once again be warmed
and stirred into activity. Like Ignatius Loyola he did
not so much have a struggle with the establishment as

such but only a burning desire to help it become by way
of manifestation all that it already was by way of promise.

The key effect which Pietism as initiated by Spener
and promoted then by many others, like Trogillus Arn-
kiel (dec.1713) and August Hermann Francke (1663-1727),
had on confirmation was the new emphasis on the subjective element as it came to expression particularly in
the renewal of the baptismal covenant and in the solemn
vows of enduring faithfulness to the Lutheran Church.
Another expression of this subjective concern is found
in the use of individual "memory verses" taken from
Scripture and assigned to each confirmand in a manner
almost reminiscent of the personal and directive pro-
phecy mentioned in Scripture (1 Tim.1:18-19a; Acts 13:
1-3). One also reads of efforts to bring the children
to "holy tears" and to an expression in their own words
of their personal faith rather than simply by use of
the more objective and traditional declarations of the
corporate faith of the church.[17]

Although this "pietistic" understanding of confirmation has often been subjected to severe criticism by
the more traditionalist elements in the Lutheran Church,
one would have to admit that apart from its excesses it
did discover a lost element of the New Testament witness
regarding "confirmation." There the confirming Spirit
of God is indeed related to subjective experience, although this experience is not so much ritualistically
and emotionally contrived as it is "waited for" in
faith-full prayer and obedience. Thus the subjective
experience occurs in the God-given answer to such prayer and obedience rather than in the emotional release
engendered by certain human activities, God-directed
though they might be. Nevertheless, pietistic confirmation seems to have left an ineradicable effect on
the practice, if not the theology, of confirmation in
the Lutheran Church and those churches closely touched
by it.

One of the churches touched by the pietistic movement in Lutheranism was the Methodist Church as founded
by John Wesley (1703-91). A committed Anglican, he had
a "conversion experience" while reading Luther's Pre-
face to the Epistle to the Romans. Thereupon he made
contact with the "Herrnhut Community" of Count N.L.von
Zinzendorf (1700-1760) in East Saxony, who for his part
had been deeply influenced by the Lutheran Pietist
A.H. Francke. Like other German Pietists Zinzendorf
had no particular desire to leave the Lutheran Church;

and similarly Wesley had no desire to leave the Anglican Church, but a lack of receptivity to his "Methodist societies within the Church of England" finally led to a separation four years after his death. Wesley had preached a simple gospel of grace for the forgiveness of sin and a disciplined quest for sanctification. Though he for the most part retained Anglican doctrinal standards, he nevertheless dropped all theological tests for church membership and required only a personal profession of faith. And when he revised the Book of Common Prayer for the novel circumstances of his American followers, he interestingly omitted the Order of Confirmation.[18] For Wesley, also, confirmation had become an experience rather than a rite, prepared for in the heart rather than in the head.

IV Confirmation after Rationalism and Revivalism

It is generally assumed that under the influence of Rationalism, confirmation grew in importance as baptism was minimized. This development is related to another assumption, namely, that the Pietists had underminded the importance of the Word and sacraments and shifted the emphasis to Christian experience.[19] Undoubtedly there are important elements of truth in these assumptions but usually they are stated with but little sensitivity to the quite legitimate concerns being registered both in Pietism and in Rationalism and with little acknowledgment of nuances in the thinking of representatives of these tendencies which would forbid such crude generalizations.

For instance, it has been stated that Georg Friedrich Seiler (1733-1807) was a late Pietist who was already affected by Rationalism and that he advocated confirmation as a substitute for baptism.[20] Subsequent research, however, has determined that his statement describing confirmation as "a baptism without water" was never intended to undermine infant baptism but rather formed part of his apologetic for it.[21] Accordingly, we must exercise caution when interpreting representatives of theological traditions with which we are only superficially familiar and with which we find ourselves out of sympathy.

Perhaps much of the difficulty at this point has come as a result of inadequate theological categories to express paradoxical and dialectical relationships. The pendulum image simply cannot do justice to the fulness of the biblical teaching on the relationship be-

tween entities such as grace and works, sacrament and
sacrifice, unilateral and bilateral covenants, and
finally, baptism and confirmation.[22] A Seiler's teaching on confirmation cannot be simply stated in terms of
a swing of the pendulum from baptism to confirmation.
The relationship between the two is more dialectically
complicated than that. And so we must also ask whether
F.D.E. Schleiermacher (1768-1834) really intended to
undermine God's grace when he attacked the absolute
value of baptism without confirmation or whether he
was instead simply laboring under a terrible inadequacy
of expression, searching as he was to give legitimate
attention to dimensions of reality neglected in more
commonly accepted orthodox formulations.[23]

It was this problem which Sören Kierkegaard (1813-
1855) sensed and which he tried to resolve with his
category of paradox, but judging from his treatment of
the relationship between baptism and confirmation in
his Attack upon "Christendom" (1854-55), he came up
with little of positive value but could only complain
that from where he stood "Confirmation then is easily
seen to be far deeper nonsense than infant baptism
. . . ."[24] Such a statement might stand as a specific
corrective but it contributes nothing substantive to
the Church's teaching either on baptism or on confirmation.

What seems to have happened in the confirmation
practice developed under the influence of Rationalsim,
however, is that certain legitimate Christian consider-
ations were emphatically reinstated after having been
sorely neglected during the hundreds of years of prac-
ticing infant baptism with a subsequent sacramentally
understood confirmation. In the sixteenth century
Erasmus had focused attention upon conscious human responsibility in his promotion of a renewal of baptismal vows at confirmation. Luther had then brought
this concern to expression by relating confirmation to
the private confession of sins and reception of absolution with the laying on of hands. Bucer developed
it still further by linking confirmation with a vow of
faithfulness not only to Christ but also to a particular discipline within a local expression of Christ's
body. Pietists wanted to make sure that all of these
personal expressions of assuming responsibility were
really from the heart and not merely intellectual game-
playing, so they linked all of the above to a conversion experience. And, finally, Rationalism provided
a more highly sophisticated ritualistic context within
which one could help bring to expression this conscious

assumption of adult responsibility. The line of development is clear enough, but unfortunately it was too much like the swing of a pendulum which after Luther more and more began to obscure the objective given from which it was coming.

Rationalism developed the following practices as a ritual framework for confirmation:

1) a highly festive atmosphere comparable to a birthday celebration;

2) the vow was often called an oath, giving it a greater eschatological and emotional dimension;

3) the personal "memory verses" were often taken from proverb-like secular, moralistic sayings rather than from the biblical promises;

4) after the confirmand's consecration he was encouraged to go to his parents and in an emotion-filled moment ask their forgiveness and blessing;

5) certain civic, social, and economic privileges began to be associated with confirmation.[25]

Thus the entire framework for Rationalism's confirmation had the net effect of enhancing the sense that the confirmand was taking a decisive step in the assumption of adult responsibilities. It was, no doubt, a Christian notion which suggested that babes in Christ were to mature in their understanding of Christian discipleship (Hebr.5:11—6:8). But it is questionable whether Rationalism adequately expressed the dialectical connection between the origin of new life in Christ through baptism and its unfolding in what could be called confirmation. Rationalism, when at its worst, gave instead the impression that the new start began with confirmation, and this when the confirmand subjectively dared to step over the line into self-conscious adulthood.

And this is why we can speak of Revivalism in the same breath with Rationalism. Although it would seem that the two have little or nothing in common, with Rivivalism letting go and letting God and Rationalism forgetting God and letting man, such crude generalizations miss the mark. Christian Rationalism did not forget God; it simply emphasized that the way to God was crucially linked with a self-conscious expression

of adult responsibility and commitment on the part of
God's creatures. Christian Revivalism, on the other
hand, did not simply "let go" and trust God's promises,
but it had its own techniques of helping Christians
warm up to God and these techniques also involved assuming certain self-conscious expressions of adult responsibility and commitment. To document this, we will
have to take a closer look at the dynamics of Revivalism.

Revivalism arose as Puritans, for whom the main
business of education was to prepare children for conversion, discovered that professions of conversion were
less and less forthcoming.[26] As a movement it was
largely the fruit of the preaching of men like Jonathan
Edwards (1703-58) and George Whitefield (1714-70),
though both preachers discouraged the excessive emotionalism (dramatic preaching, abnormal bodily excite-
ment, groanings, etc.) which soon marked the revival.
However, stress was laid on visible evidences of conversion, and those who persistently did not manifest
such tokens of inward grace, whether clergy or laymen,
were openly suspected of unregeneracy.

Edwards agreed to a doctrine of "preparation for
salvation." Even though he uncompromisingly emphasized God's grace as the source of salvation, his non-
sacramental understanding of that grace made it difficult for him to distinguish in any practical and pastoral way the prevenience of God's unsolicited grace
on the one hand, from the cooperative participation
expressed in man's various responses to God's Word in
both law and gospel on the other. Thus the subjectivism inherent in the Rationalist understanding of confirmation had its analogy in the Revivalist understanding of conversion, although the former advocated an
emotionalism more consistently rooted in and normed by
reason than did the latter.[27] Whereas the Revivalist
emotions could be periodically stirred and renewal
thereby rekindled, the Rationalist, with his emotions
tied more intimately to a step taken once for all in
connection with maturing intellect, could less readily
experience a repetition of the moment of his confirmation.

V   Confirmation after Renewal Attempts in the Nine-
    teenth Century

Rationalism and Revivalism had carried the development of confirmation about as far as it could go in

its pendulum swing from objective medieval sacramental-
ism to subjective Christian self-discovery experiences.
Rationalism tied that experience particularly to something going on in the head whereas Revivalism tied it
to something happening in the heart, but either way
it was a movement toward increased subjectivism. The
nineteenth century, however, revealed a certain unea-
siness about this subjectivism and it struggled once
again to put down some roots, yet without losing what
had been developing in the less restrictive atmosphere
of the preceding three hundred years.

F.D.E. Schleiermacher coming out of a home deeply
affected by Pietism and an education heavily laced with
Kantian moralism and Schlegelian romanticism looked for
rootage and found it in what he called "the feeling of
absolute dependence." This was a "feeling" far different from the daily ups and downs of one's emotional
life. It had staying power since it was rooted in the
"absolute," at least, that is what Schleiermacher
thought he had discovered.

Horace Bushnell (1802-76), a Congregational divine,
was the pioneer of liberal theology in New England. He
reacted against the Revivalist emphasis on individual
conversion triggered in the midst of personal crisis
and saw religious life instead as a growth process emerging from "the secret seeds of grace" sown consistently
though perhaps inconspiciously within the Church as
Christian community. He blurred the line between nature and super-nature, understanding the objective grace
of God to be operative already in man's natural environ-
ment as seen through Christian eyes rather than more re-
strictively in the particularities of revelation as defined by Christian tradition. His book, Christian
Nurture (1847), by its very title wished to combat an
understanding of grace which individualized and particularized and to offer instead a more broadly based and
objective foundation for Christian existence.[28]

In Germany, Lutheranism was experiencing a renewed
appreciation for its confessional heritage, particularly through the contributions of the Erlangen school of
theologians. These men expressed a concern for a more
explicit connection between the grace of sacramental
baptism, the grace of sacramental communion, and the
response to and expectation of such grace in the rites
surrounding confirmation.[29] It was a matter of the
head and the heart as well as of the subjective and the
objective.

Perhaps it would not lead astray to summarize the nineteenth century as one in which the metaphors of growth and development were gradually finding their place along side the metaphors of crisis and conversion. The closer the church came to rediscovering the canonicity of both and the particular dialectical relationship between the two, the closer it also came to solving the problematical relationship between baptism and confirmation. But it was when the New Testament charismata once again broke in upon the scene, and especially when these were experienced by Christians not so much as marking the point of their being "born again" but as "confirmation" of who they in fact were as born again Christians, that greater clarity began to emerge and the pendulum image could slowly be replaced by the image of the flower. But that is the story of confirmation in the twentieth century.

Footnotes

1Judith Tydings, Gathering a People (Plainfield: Logos, 1977), pp.251-268. In a very interesting appendix Tydings briefly makes some comparisons between the Spiritual Exercises of St. Ignatius Loyola and a booklet used in charismatic circles, The Life in the Spirit Seminars Team Manual, which latter in turn has made its own contribution to an understanding of confirmation in Roman Catholic circles. See Rev. Charles Antekeier, Van and Janet Vandagriff, Confirmation: The Power of the Spirit. A Charismatic Preparation Program for Youth, their Parents and Sponsors (Notre Dame: Ave Maria, 1972).

2Robert E. McNally, S.J., "Ignatius Loyola," in Reformers in Profile, B.A. Gerrish, ed. (Philadelphia: Fortress, 1967), p.254.

3Walter Nigg, Warriors of God: The Great Religious Orders and their Founders, tr. Mary Ilford (London: Secker and Warburg, 1959), p.353.

4McNally, op. cit., pp.243; 248-251.

5Ibid., p.238; Nigg, op. cit., pp.322-323.

6Tydings, op. cit., pp.259; 261.

7McNally, op. cit., pp.236-237; Nigg, op.cit., pp.336-338.

[8]Nigg, op. cit., pp.348-351; McNally, op. cit., pp.247-248; 253-255.

[9]McNally, op. cit., pp.252-253; Nigg, op. cit., pp. 342-343; Repp, op. cit., pp.107-112.

[10]Daniel B. Stevick, "Christian Initiation; Post-Reformation to the Present Era," in Made, Not Born, pp.106-107.

[11]Ibid., pp.107-108; Robert H. Fischer, "Confirmation Outside the Anglican Tradition," in Confirmation, K. B. Cully, ed., pp.41-43.

[12]Robert H. Fischer, op. cit., pp.42; 44.

[13]Repp, op. cit., pp.61-68, esp. p. 64.

[14]Ibid., pp.68-69; also Dale Drown, Understanding Pietism (Grand Rapids: Eerdmans, 1978), p.12, and Richard F. Lovelace, Dynamics of Spiritial Life: An Evangelical Theology of Renewal (Downers Grove: Inter-Varsity, 1979), pp.25-60.

[15]Repp, op. cit., p.69; also G.W.H. Lampe, "The Relation of Baptism and Confirmation," in Confirmation, K. B. Cully, ed., pp.70-72; 81-83.

[16]Repp, op. cit., pp.69-70.

[17]Ibid., pp.71-72.

[18]Robert H. Fischer, op. cit., p.44.

[19]Repp, op. cit., pp.76-77.

[20]Ibid., p.77.

[21]Ottfried Jordahn, Georg Friedrich Seilers Beitrag zur Praktischen Theologie der kirchlichen Aufklärung (Nürnberg: Selbstverlag des Vereins für bayerische Kirchengeschichte, 1970), pp.215-216.

[22]Repp, op. cit., pp.107-108.

[23]Ibid., p.77; Friedrich Schleiermacher, The Christian Faith, Vol. 2, H. R. Mackintosh and J. S. Stewart, eds. (New York: Harper and Row, 1963), pp.626-638.

[24]Repp, op. cit., pp.87-88; Sören Kierkegaard, Attack upon "Christendom," tr. Walter Lowrie (Boston:

Beacon, 1944), p.218.

25Repp, op. cit., pp.78-81.

26Robert H. Fischer, op. cit., p.45.

27Conrad Cherry, <u>The Theology of Jonathan Edwards</u>:
<u>A Reappraisal</u> (Garden City:Doubleday, 1966), pp.60-68;
164-176.

28Robert H. Fischer, op. cit., pp.46-47; also Martin E. Marty, <u>Righteous Empire: The Protestant Experience in America</u> (New York: Dial, 1970), pp.193-194.

29Repp, op. cit., pp.84-92.

Chapter Six

CONFIRMATION IN THE TWENTIETH CENTURY:
THE CHANGING SHAPE OF THE QUESTION

The effect of the Sixteenth Century Reformation on
confirmation had been to reverse the process whereby it
had become an independent sacrament. Although it succeeded in doing this only in that portion of the church
which is called Protestant, the effect was universally
felt in the church. Where confirmation continued to
be thought of as a sacrament, the element of human responsibility was nevertheless reemphasized; where it
ceased to be understood as a sacrament, the debate regarding how confirmation could be structured so as to
allow it to give helpful expression to human responsibility began in particular earnest. In the succeeding
four hundred years this responsibility has been interpreted variously as touching specifically a person's
will, his mind, or his emotions. But a "holistic" understanding did not seem to be forthcoming - neither
one which effectively integrated will, mind, and emotions, nor one which succeeded in integrating sacrament and sacrifice as God's gift and human responsibility. Inevitably, differing emphases were interpreted as conflicting, and confirmation became a matter
of confessionalistic dispute and polemics. Differences
became so numerous and so intense that their resolution
seemed to require an intervention on God's part - and
this is precisely what happened.

Only now are we beginning to realize the extent to
which God intervened when he allowed the explosive rise
of Pentecostalism at the beginning of the twentieth
century. The story has been often repeated and we need
not do so here.[1] But the point dare not be overlooked.
The renewal in our own time of the Pentecostal experience as it had been attested throughout the Book of
Acts suddenly set before the Church the possibility
which Calvin had insisted was the only valid "confirmation" but which he also insisted was limited to the
apostolic generation.[2] So threatening was this possibility of a confirmation "not made with hands" but
which instead remained in God's sovereign control that
the church for the most part called it madness or de-
monic or both.[3]

Any fair assessment of the rise of Pentecostalism
would have to admit that the Corinthian heresy has

stalked it like a shadow. Its development occurred too
exclusively as a fringe movement of the church at best
and as divisive sectarianism at worst. But that there
was also something oddly like the New Testament about
it, no one could in good conscience deny.[4] To release
that "something" into what are sometimes called the
"mainstream denominations," a second intervention on
God's part apparently became necessary and this occurred with the rise of what at first was called "Neo-
Pentecostalism" but which later preferred to be termed
the "Charismatic Movement" or "Charismatic Renewal."[5]
Here self-consciously "orthodox" Episcopalians, Lutherans, Presbyterians, Roman Catholics, and others experienced Pentecostal manifestations previously found
only among what now came to be called "classical Pentecostals." However, these "new Pentecostals" made con-
certed efforts to integrate their charismatic experience with the fuller tradition of biblical teaching
and sacramental practice found in the historical churches. All of this has forced, at least for some in
the mainline denominations, an encounter between traditional confirmation practices and the confirming
experiences of charismatic manifestations.

Meanwhile two other influences had touched the
mainline churches in a way which succeeded in opening
them up to evaluating their by now traditional confirmation practices. The one influence was the so-called
"liturgical renewal" and the other the effect of the
social sciences on pedagogical practices, including
those in the church.

In the following we shall describe and assess the
changing shape of the question of confirmation today
as it is confronted by these three influences: the
liturgical renewal, the pedagogical renewal, and the
charismatic renewal.

    I   Confirmation and the Liturgical Renewal

The twentieth century was not only marked at its
very beginning by the rise of Pentecostalism, but it
also brought with it a movement already in process
known as the liturgical renewal. However, it is especially since the end of World War I that this movement has gathered ecumenical momentum and widely affected the churches, particularly the Roman Catholic
Church through the decisions set in motion by the
Second Vatican Council (1962-1965). The reforms in
the so-called initiatory practices of the church is

the point where our question of confirmation is most
directly touched.

How, specifically, has Vatican II affected the theology and practice of confirmation?

This Council gathered together the results of de-
cades of study relating to the initiatory rites of the
church and translated them into official directives for
changes in liturgical practice.[6] There was a recognition that confirmation as an independent sacrament had
succeeded in overshadowing baptism as an initiatory
rite, a situation which could not be harmonized with
the New Testament witness nor the tradition of the
early church.[7] It had been the particular burden of
the liturgical renewal to implement such changes in
the practical theology of the church as would once a-
gain release the dynamic which baptism seems to have
had in the New Testament and in the church of the first
three centuries. Whereas the charismatic renewal, as
we shall see, has expected to find this baptismal dy-
namism released through faith and prayer and the consequent manifestation of the charismata, the liturgical renewal has sought to release it by the discipline
of a renewed catechumenate and the experiential impact
of a renewed ritual.[8]

It is of interest to note how in the liturgical
renewal the release of this spiritual dynamic is tied
first of all to establishing _adult_ baptism as the most
traditional _norm_ of baptismal polity and then to the
proliferation or maximalization of sacramental _ritual_
as the incarnational means.[9] _Infant_ baptism is not so
much rejected as it is minimized by terminology such as
"benign abnormality,"[10] the suggestion that it may be
the wrong rite for the right idea,[11] and the rejection
of original guilt even while maintaining the notion of
original sin.[12]

Although one finds in the interpretation of these
renewed initiation rites a pointed rejection of sectarian and elitist thinking (and a tendency to hang
these labels on those involved in charismatic renewal),[13] there is, nevertheless, a distinction made even
here between "Christians" and the "Faithful," but one
which need not be sectarian or elitist in effect.[14]
It is the distinction between "new Christians," those
just enrolled in the catechumenate, and fully "initiated Christians," that is, those who have been baptized, confirmed, and communed and who are therefore
the "Faithful." This distinction is trying to get at

the same problem as is suggested by the allusion to
"sacramental community" and "intentional community"
above.[15]

But, more specifically, how is confirmation understood in these post Vatican II initiatory rites? The
aim of the revised rite is that "the intimate connection
which this sacrament has with the whole of Christian
initiation should be more lucidly set forth." It is
also stated that "the faithful are born anew by baptism,
strengthened by the sacrament of confirmation, and finally are sustained by the food of eternal life in the
eucharist."[16] Again: "In the sacrament of confirmation
the apostles and the bishops who are their successors
hand on to the baptized the special gift of the Holy
Spirit, promised by Christ the Lord and poured out upon
the apostles at Pentecost. Thus the initiation in the
Christian life is completed so that believers are
strengthened by power from heaven, made true witnesses
of Christ in word and deed, and bound more closely to
the Church."[17] Finally, it is taught that the anointing with chrism, more so than the laying on of hands,
and the words "Accipe Signaculum Doni Spiritus Sancti,"
that is, "Be sealed with the gift of the Holy Spirit,"
are the means whereby this sacrament is conferred.[18]

Commentators upon these rites recognize that there
remain unevennesses which will have to be worked out in
time and through use.[19] The most disturbing tension is
that existing between what seems to be the urging to
unify the initiatory sacraments by postponing them to
adulthood and the traditional chronological separation
resulting from infant baptism and adolescent confirmation. For instance, Aidan Kavanagh argues for the
greatest possible expression of a unified rite, whereas
Günter Biemer pushes for greater sensitivity to developmental psychology and intentional alteration of behav-
iour, even calling into question the new and broader
application of the term "initiation."[20] One is also
tempted to ask whether it might not be what seems to be
Kavanagh's outspokenly anti-charismatic bias which
prompts him to interpret Pentecost not as "the special
time for confirmation but as the next most appropriate
time for baptism in its fulness after Easter itself."[21]
He dares to say this in spite of what the official rites
explicitly state regarding the connection between confirmation and Pentecost.[22] Yet Kavanagh's dismay at
what he calls a "dislocation in sacramental sequence
by separating confirmation from baptism and inserting
holy communion between the two,"[23] does not seem to
recognize the same supposed "dislocation" in the New

Testament witness to the initiatory experience of the
Apostles. For them too Maundy Thursday preceded Pentecost.

Although these developments in liturgical renewal
within Roman Catholicism are perhaps those which most
profoundly affect other churches,[24] the newly legis-
lated changes had already all been anticipated within
the debate taking place among the leadership in the
Anglican communion.[25] The crucial stage of the ex-
change was triggered by the writings of Gregory Dix
(1946) and L. S. Thornton (1954), who on the one hand
made the strongest possible case for confirmation as a
distinct sacrament necessary for salvation, and G.W.M.
Lampe (1951), who on the other hand severely criticized
the absorption of the Holy Spirit in a ritual of confirmation and called instead for the rediscovery of the
gift of the Holy Spirit in baptism. From this debate
emerged several trends, the first of which has already
received official formulation in the new Roman Catholic
"Rites" and the rest of which are still at various
points in the discussion stage. They are: the restora-
tion of the ancient catechumenate; the rejection of infant guilt; a service of child dedication (that is, as
the first stage of the catechumenate).[26]

Some Lutherans, it seems, have also taken their
cues for confirmation from developments rooted in the
liturgical renewal, although with typically Lutheran
modifications. Eugene L. Brand has been their articulate spokesman, making a strong case for a revision of
the initiatory rites which would correct the minimalist
and reductionist attitude toward ritual which had developed out of the Reformation's traditional emphasis on
water and the Word.[27] However, unlike the Roman Catholic Kavanagh, he continues to make a strong case for
infant baptism even while acknowledging that the theological norm must remain adult baptism. This norm is
brought to expression by insisting upon a single rite
for baptism, the adult-type questions remaining also in
the baptism of infants as a reminder of that into which
it is in faith expected that the child will by God's
grace grow.[28] He strongly opposes indiscriminate baptism and emphasizes pastoral and congregational care
for those baptized, defending emergency baptisms not so
much for strictly theological reasons as for pastoral
reasons.[29]

What does the new Lutheran "Rites of Confirmation"
growing out of this background look like? Actually,
it doesn't look too much like traditional Lutheran

"Confirmation." Instead, this new rite is called
"Affirmation of Baptism," the term "Confirmation" ap-
pearing in the finer print only.[30] Brand himself,
following a suggestion of an Episcopal liturgical conference meeting in Amarillo, Texas, in 1974, advises
Lutherans that the term "Confirmation" be "dropped from
future forms, titles, and, so far as possible, from dis-
cussions relating to Christian Initiation."[31] He shares
the general and appropriate anxiety about a confirmation practice which results in somehow reducing baptism
and its consequences to a "mere."[32] Thus he insists with
Luther that baptism is more than a mere "ritual moment,"
that it is tied to the future of one's life for its
"completion" (Luther: "until fully baptized").[33]

     Brand is far more open than Kavanagh to develop-
ments within the charismatic renewal, but he does not
seem to make the direct connection, which we have docu-
mented as being a consistent New Testament perspective,
between confirmation (experientially, not ritually,
understood) and the manifestation of the charismata.[34]
He does sense the importance of faith as the means of
perceiving and receiving the grace of baptism, but he
is strongly disposed against speaking of this faith in
terms of "personal and individual decision."[35] Thus
he fails to take seriously enough another renewal which
is affecting theology simultaneously with the liturgical renewal and the charismatic renewal, namely, the
pedagogical renewal with its contribution in the area
of theology known as "faith development."[36]

          II Confirmation and the Pedagogical Renewal

     A leading exponent of the "faith development" in-
terpretation of the Christian life has been the Lutheran, Thomas A. Droege. His book on Self-Realization
and Faith employs the developmental principle (particularly as expounded by Erik Erikson) as a cricital tool
in examining varying doctrines of faith and then as providing a practical and constructive resolution of the
ancient controversy concerning the relationship between
baptism and confirmation.[37] In doing so he joins Günter Biemer in the struggle of a "pastoral-anthropomor-
phic" conception of the sacraments against a "dogmatico-
ecclesiological" conception such as is represented by
the leading voices within liturgical renewal.[38] But by
insisting on speaking of the relationship between baptism and confirmation not merely in terms of psychological development but rather in terms of a distinct but

not separate faith development, he avoids falling into
the secularist trap against which Kent S. Knutson had
so eloquently warned.[39] Nevertheless, Droege comes up
with results which draw forth the ire of men like Kavanagh, who would term as "relentless ritual rationalism"
what Droege has preferred to call the 'intuitive wis-
dom within the church to discern significant developmental milestones in the lives of individuals" - the
Rite of Confirmation and its relation to faith's "self-
realization" being one of them.[40]

     But just what is meant by "faith development"
according to Droege and how does it help us relate baptism and confirmation?

          . . . self-reception and self-realization can be
          regarded as two separate descriptions of the self
          at two different stages of the life cycle. It
          is possible in this way to acknowledge that faith
          has its beginning in God's naming the child as
          His own in Baptism while at the same time affirm-
          ing that there is a process of becoming in which
          faith realizes its potential for obedience, com-
          mitment, self-understanding, etc.[41]

          . . . the distinction between Baptism and con-
          firmation is a distinction in the self at two
          different points of development. It is this
          notion of development that provides the key to
          the continuities and discontinuities between Bap-
          tism and confirmation, between self-reception and
          self-realization. Although it is God who con-
          firms the gift already bestowed in fullness at
          the time of Baptism, it is man who receives the
          gift and realizes its benefits through his being
          and becoming.[42]

     Droege's understanding of "faith development"
seems to have better support in classical Lutheran tradition than he himself realizes. In Lutheranism's
fundamental exposition of the meaning of "justification
by faith," Melanchthon uses at least four different
words to describe faith - one more than Droege allows
when reminding us of the "classical definition" of the
act of faith based upon the adult model: _notitia_ (knowledge), _assensus_ (assent), and _fiducia_ (trust).[43] The
important designation for faith employed by Melanchthon,
but not noted by Droege, is _acceptio_ (reception), which
particularly in its verbal and passive form Melanchthon
(and Luther too) frequently uses to describe faith.[44]
It is important to note, however, that Melanchthon does

not schematize these four descriptions according to
some supposed adult model, thereby leaving the question of possible schematization according to a contemporary developmental model open, for example: reception, trust, knowledge, assent. But the overall emphasis of Melanchthon seems to fall on faith as reception even more so than as trust, an emphasis which
Droege himself both seems to appreciate and yet criticizes because of its supposed "purely passive" character.[45]

Droege's concept of "developmental faith" and his
description of baptism as "self-reception" and confirmation as "self-realization" allow him to appreciate
the chronological separation of baptism and confirmation as it had developed already by the fifth century,
but to do so without separating their intimate theological relationship. His understanding of confirmation is one which values what among Roman Catholics
had come to be termed the "sacrament of maturity" -
a concept which Kavanagh criticizes as an invasion or
manipulation of "the Christian" by "the civil."[46] The
consequence of Kavanagh's approach is the conclusion
that "the form, place, and meaning of the sealing
[confirmation] have absolutely nothing to do with the
physical _or_ social _or_ emotional _or_ intellectual _or_ even
spiritual 'age' of the initiate."[47] The consequence
of Droege's approach, on the other hand, is the conclusion that confirmation would best occur at the end of
the tenth grade (ages 15-16) and first communion would
best be delayed in order to occur at that same time,
thus expressing in _action_ what both the community and
confirmand have just expressed through _words_ in the
confirmation service.[48]

How best can we analyze and summarize this difference between representatives of liturgical renewal
and representatives of pedagogical renewal relative to
the meaning and practice of confirmation? It would appear that for Kavanagh, confirmation should basically
be a "ritual experience" - one which would bring to
robust expression the baptismal fullness of the Christian initiate's identity with Christ and the community
of believers. For Droege, on the other hand, confirmation should basically be a "faith/self-realization
experience" - one which would employ an appropriate
ritual to bring into public focus the Christian initiate's more fully developed baptismal faith.

But I am left with these questions: Can ecclesial
ritual (even when it includes the catechumenate as

described by Kavanagh) be the guarantee whereby one can
be assured that the baptized have been (more) fully
initiated into Christ and the community of faith? Or
can biological age (even when Droege presupposes catechetical instruction with an appropriate concluding
rite) be such a guarantee? Can there by any guarantee
of such full (Eph.3:14-19; Rom.15:18-19, 29) initiation
other than the "guarantee" (arrabon) of the Spirit in
our hearts (2 Cor.1:22; Eph.1:13-14), the "first-fruit"
(aparkee) of the Spirit being found in the fervent cry
"Abba! Father!" (Rom.8:15-16; Gal.4:6), and in the
"sighs too deep for words" (Rom.8:22-27), and the "confirmation" (bebaiōsis) of this Gospel being expressed
through the manifestation of the fruit and gifts (charismata) of the Spirit (Phil.1:6-11; Hebr.2:3-4; 1 Cor.1:
4-7; 12:4-11; etc.)?

Liturgical renewal and pedagogical renewal have
clearly enriched our understanding of "Confirmation"
insofar as its meaning is tied to Easter, whether ritually or faith-developmentally, but neither has helped
us understand it from the perspective of the Pentecostal
experience of the Apostles and those who like the Apostles in faith-full obedience and prayer "waited for the
promise of the Father." And so it is to the charismatic
renewal and its contribution to an understanding of
"Confirmation" to which we must now turn.

III   Confirmation and the Charismatic Renewal

Since Pentecost is, of course, intimately related
to Easter, there is no way in which Easter can be left
behind and exchanged for a supposedly newer and better
revelation - that of Pentecost. However, it is not a
new experience in the Church to find that Pentecost
either becomes detached from Easter and one thus hears
of "spiritual renewal" which is not unbrokenly tied to
the cross and resurrection of Jesus (something which
John's Gospel seems to wish to avoid);[49] nor is one
surprised to hear of Pentecost simply being absorbed
into the Easter event in such a way that the Scriptural
witness to the distinctive blessings of Pentecost is
anxiously muted (something which Luke-Acts seems to
resist).[50]

Luther also on occasion was moved with great pas-
sion and vigor to resist the reduction of the salvation
event to an Easter which did not necessarily provoke a
personal Pentecost - Pentecost being understood as a

spiritual gift-receiving which derived from Easter but
not automatically so. It had to be provoked by the
"preaching of Pentecost." For instance, Luther wrote
in his treatise "On the Councils and the Church" (1539):

> That is what my Antinomians, too, are doing
> today, who are preaching beautifully and (as
> I cannot but think) with real sincerity about
> Christ's grace, about the forgiveness of sin
> and whatever else can be said about the doc-
> trine of redemption. But they flee as if it
> were the very devil the consequence that they
> should tell the people about the third arti-
> cle of sanctification, that is, of the new
> life in Christ. They think one should not
> frighten or trouble the people, but rather
> always preach comfortingly about grace and
> forgiveness of sins in Christ, and under no
> circumstances use these or similar words,
> "Listen! You want to be a Christian and at
> the same time remain an adulterer, a whore-
> monger, a drunken swine, arrogant, covetous,
> a usurer, envious, vindictive, malicious,
> etc.!" Instead they say, "Listen! Though
> you are an adulterer, a whoremonger, a miser,
> or other kind of sinner, if you but believe,
> you are saved, and you need not fear the law.
> Christ has fulfilled it all!"

> Tell me, my dear man, is that not granting
> the premise [Easter] and denying the conclu-
> sion [Pentecost] ? It is, indeed, taking a-
> way Christ and bringing him to nought at the
> same time he is most beautifully proclaimed!
> And it is saying yes and no to the same thing.
> For there is no such Christ that died for sin-
> ners who do not, after the forgiveness of sins,
> desist from sins and lead a new life . . . .
> They may be fine Easter preachers, but they
> are very poor Pentecost preachers, for they do
> not preach de sanctificatione et vivificatione
> Spiritus Sancti, "about the sanctification by
> the Holy Spirit," but solely about the redemp-
> tion of Jesus Christ, although Christ (whom
> they so extoll so highly, and rightly so) is
> Christ, that is, he has purchased redemption
> from sin and death so that the Holy Spirit
> might transform us out of the old Adam into
> new men . . . . . Christ did not earn only gra-
> tia, "grace", for us, but also donum, "the
> gift of the Holy Spirit," so that we might

have not only forgiveness of, but also cessation
of, sin. Now he who does not abstain from sin,
but persists in his evil life, must have a different Christ, that of the Antinomians; the real
Christ is not there, even if all the angels would
cry, "Christ! Christ!" He must be damned with this,
his new Christ.

. . . But our Antinomians fail to see that they
are preaching Christ without and against the Holy
Spirit because they propose to let the people continue in their old ways and still pronounce them
saved. And yet logic, too, implies that a Christian should either have the Holy Spirit and lead
a new life, or know that he has no Christ.51

Although Luther in this particular passage limits
his understanding of the Spirit's "gift" to the Pentecostal expectation of the "fruit of the Spirit," Karlfried Froelich has pointed out that Luther frequently
preached on 1 Corinthians 12:1-11 as the appointed E-
pistle lesson for the 10th Sunday after Trinity and
that there are extant transcripts of at least four ser-
mons in which Luther dealt with the "charismatic gifts"
as Pentecostal expressions still to be expected and experienced today as "confirmation" of the Gospel.52
Luther's "Pentecostalism" cannot be rooted out by reading him through the eyes of a Calvin or a Chemnitz with
their dispensationalist tendencies or by limiting one's
familiarity with his theology to his anti-enthusiastic
utterances.53 Nor can we domesticate Luther's Pentecostal expectations by imagining that he could only
identify with "the crowd" and not with "the disciples"
of the first Pentecost.54 Luther could identify not
only with the disciples but with Christ himself, for
he wrote: "If a Christian has the faith, he shall have
the power to do these signs . . . . For a Christian has
equal power with Christ, is one cake with him . . . .
Where there is a Christian, there is therefore the power to do such signs even now if it is necessary . . .
to proclaim the Word of God and to confirm it by miracles."55

From all this we can conclude that Pentecost will
be experienced to the extent that it is preached and
believed. If Christian preaching reduces Pentecost to
the simple exhortation: "Repent and be baptized every
one of you in the name of Jesus Christ for the forgiveness of your sins; and you shall receive the gift of
the Holy Spirit. For the promise is to you and to your
children and to all that are far off, every one whom

the Lord our God calls to him" (Acts 2:38-39), that is
most likely the extent (tremendous in itself!) to which
Pentecost will be experienced. However, if we can make
all the Apostle Paul's words our own and say with him,
". . . for I did not shrink from declaring to you the
whole counsel of God" (Acts 20:27), and ". . . concerning spiritual gifts, brethren, I do not want you to be
uninformed" (1 Cor.12:1), and "make love your aim, and
earnestly desire the spiritual gifts, especially that
you may prophesy" (1 Cor.14:1), the evidence seems to
say that we can expect much more of Pentecost to occur
in our lives than many of us have been led to believe.
If we would allow our faith to be instructed and expanded by the full range of the New Testament witness to
the Pentecostal gifts of the Holy Spirit, we could once
again more decisively and more broadly experience "Confirmation" as it was before it was so radically reduced
to a liturgical ritual or to a secularized rite of mat-
uration. The "minimalism" of our expectations has seriously limited what the Holy Spirit can do in our lives
(Matt.13:58).

But why should this be the case? Is the Holy
Spirit not the third person of the Holy Trinity and
therefore sovereign God? Does he not blow where _he_
wills and not merely where _we_ allow him (Jn.3:8)?
It is true, as John says, that our spiritual _birth_ is
not a matter of our willing but of God's (Jn.1:12-13).
However, after God has given us this new birth in Holy
Baptism (Jn.3:5), how much does he impose his will upon
us for our growth and how much does he wait for our
will to be in tune with his before he exercises it?

Pentecostalism has long been aware that there is
a "cost" in "Pentecost." Certain segments of Chris-
tianity, which have picked up on the theme of God's
"unconditional grace" manifested in Jesus Christ, have
tended to sneer not only at this demonstration of ety-
mological ignorance, but have felt compelled to reject
its apparent Pelagian or simoniacal theology as well.
However, this criticism fails to recognize what Bonhoeffer has called "costly grace" - a grace so strong
that it is miraculously able to change egocentric lov-
ers of self into people gladly and willingly ready to
pay the cost of discipleship, for "When Christ calls
a man, he bids him come and die."[56] It exposes the
inadequacy of longstanding theological shibboleths such
as "grace alone," monergism," and "unilateral covenant"
when these are detached from their dynamic Scriptural
contexts which make clear the power of God's grace to
effect in believers the "fruits of faith," a God-

trusting "synergism," and God-pleasing "bilateral covenants." The charismatic renewal is rediscovering the
proper place for the "if" in a theology of grace (Rom.11:
6; 1 Cor. 15:1-2; Hebr.3:6, 12-15; Jn.8:31). It is dis-
covering experientially what Scripture means when one
reads: "The Lord is with you, while you are with him.
If you seek him, he will be found by you, but if you
forsake him, he will forsake you" (2 Chron.15:2). "You
will seek me and find me; when you seek me with all
your heart, I will be found by you, says the Lord"
(Jer.29:13-14). "If we have died with him, we shall
also live with him; if we endure, we shall also reign
with him; if we deny him, he also will deny us; if we
are faithless, he remains faithful - for he cannot deny
himself" (2 Tim.2:11-13). "And I tell you, Ask, and it
will be given you . . . . If you then, who are evil,
know how to give good gifts to your children, how much
more will the heavenly Father give the Holy Spirit to
those who ask him" (Lk.11:9-13).

Luther was correct when he insisted that Pentecost preachers are needed, that is, preachers who have
understood the irreversible dialectical relationship
between "unconditional" and "conditional," between
"grace" and "faith," between "promise" and "fulfillment," between "Easter" and "Pentecost," between "baptism" and "confirmation." The preaching of Pentecost
is the preaching of faith-full obedience and prayer
directed to a Jesus who is not only risen (Savior) but
who is also therefore ascended to the right hand of the
Father (Lord) and from that position of "all authority"
(Matt.28:18) fulfills his promise to "baptize with the
Holy Spirit" (Acts 1:5; 2:33, 38-39) and thus not only
to "save" by way of the baptismal promise but also to
"confirm" those who believe the message by the signs
that attend it (Mk.16:16-20).

Confirmation, however, does presuppose repentance.
It is part of the "cost" of Pentecost, a gift (Acts 5:
31; 11:18) and yet a task (Acts 2:38; 3:19). God can
"confirm" only to the extent that its reception has
been prepared by repentance and faith. That is why a
repentant confession of sins and the faith-full reception of their absolution are followed by God's "confirmation" in the form of the charismata of peace and
joy (Ps.38:1-4, 18-22; 51:1-12). And this is not far
from the Reformation insight that "Confirmation" somehow is closely related to confession and absolution.[57]
Confirmation is the experience of God's grace in the
sense that Luther experienced it at the time of his
tower-discovery of the meaning of the "righteousness

of God." Of this he wrote: "I _felt_ myself to be reborn
and to have gone through open doors into paradise."[58]
If Luther's baptismal theology demands that we locate
his rebirth at his _sacramental baptism_, then his tower-
experience was a particularly powerful (with more to
follow) _confirmation_ of that rebirth - a personal appropriation by faith leading to a felt experience of the
rebirth which had earlier been baptismally conferred.

My own experience follows along the same lines.
It was the "peace and joy" experienced particularly in
connection with private confession and absolution which
established in me an appreciation for God's confirming
charismata; and when biblical instruction and the witness of other believers expanded my understanding of
the charismata so that they included not only manifestations of the "fruit of the Spirit" (Gal.5:22-23) but
also the full range of the "gifts of the Spirit"
(1 Cor.12:8-11; cf. Rom.12:6-8; 1 Pet.4:10-11), further "confirmations" were forthcoming. I was being
confirmed and simultaneously further equipped to be a
bolder and more effective witness for Christ (Lk.24:
48-49; Acts 1:4-5, 8; Jn. 20:19-23; Matt. 28:16-20).[59]

Occasionally one notes within the response of mainline churches to this understanding of "confirmation" a
critique of the emphasis it seems to place on words
like "expectancy" and the role which prayer has in trig-
gering or releasing such confirmations. Insofar as this
concern wishes to signal the danger of transforming
prayer into a "means of grace" in the same sense as
"Word and sacraments" are such means, it has its legi-
timacy, since prayer as subjective response to God's
promises is secondary, whereas the objective Word and
sacraments are primary. However, if this concern has
as its result the setting aside of the God-ordained
role prayer is to have relative to the subjective experience of grace, it is illegitimate. Biblically
speaking the charismatic renewal has recognized the important distinction between the God-given means of objectively offering grace (Word and sacraments), the
means of subjectively receiving grace (faith), and the
means of personally realizing and manifesting grace
(faithfull obedience and prayer), thus refusing to play
one word of Scripture off against another but allowing
the fullness of Scripture to come to expression.[60]
There is no doubt that Scripture attaches importance
to expectant prayer as a means of realizing the confirming gifts of the Holy Spirit (Lk.11:9-13; 1 Cor.12:31;
14:1, 12-13; 2 Cor.1:11; Acts 1:4-5, 14; etc.).[61]

One of the more traditional roles which "Confirmation" has played in church history is the signalling
of the confirmand's personal commitment to Christ and
to the local and translocal body of believers. We have
seen above how the advocates of "faith development"
have affirmed that traditional view. Participants in
charismatic renewal would lend their strong support to
this approach, adding, however, that by itself it does
not yet exhaust the New Testament possibilities for
understanding "Confirmation." In keeping with their
own understanding of the possibility of faith development,[62] they would also be willing to speak of a developing participation in the community of faith - one
which moves from sacramental community to intertional
community, but with the latter continuing to find its
roots firmly grounded in the former. For those involved in charismatic renewal, however, the development
into intentional community (confirmation understood as
a rite of maturity) would be accompanied by the kind of
expectant prayers which would invite the further manifestation of charismata to "confirm" such "faith intentions" by equipping the "initiates" with the "spiritual
gifts" necessary for mature functioning within the
"body," that it might, as the Apostle admonishes, be
the better "built up" (1 Cor.14:1-5, 12-19).[63]

There is, of course, a risk in all of this, namely,
the risk of creating a church of the elite, functioning
in high disregard for those whose "intentions" appear
less mature and explicit and whose "gifts" are ordinarily less valued. The Apostle Paul rejects out of hand
such behavior, but he does not thereby refuse to distinguish between the weak and the strong in the one body
and the "intentions" suited to each (Rom14:1-4; 15:1-6).
And he insists that healthy "growth" (development) must
become the intention of all (Eph.4:1-16; 1 Cor.3:1-15).

Interestingly, the extent is minimal to which those
involved in charismatic renewal have explicated a theology and practice of confirmation which would integrate
their own new insights, especially those involving the
experience of confirming charismata, with the Church's
more traditional catechetical practice and liturgical
Confirmation Rite. One can read of a few attempts to
do so,[64] but apparently the changes demanded by such
rethinking would be so great and so threatening that
recent renewal developments (liturgical, pedagogical,
and charismatic) have by and large occurred side by side
and often even competitively rather than integratively.[65]

Roman Catholics involved in charismatic renewal

seem to have been the most aggressive in developing a
catechetical program which integrates traditional thinking regarding confirmation with very real expectation
of charismatic manifestations in connection with the
administration of the "Sacrament of Confirmation," occasionally even calling it an "interchangeable expression" with "baptism in the Holy Spirit."[66] Judith Tydings, although she describes the _Exercises_ of Ignatius
and the _Life in the Spirit Seminars_ merely as "a tool
for evangelization, initiation and subsequent formation
of fervent Christians," uses the Ignatian device of not
directly challenging "tradition" but rather explicating
it in such a way as in effect to be engaged in a not so
subtle redefinition of confirmation as "charismatic
manifestations" rather than as "sacramental promise."
Or, if that is saying too much, hers is at least a suggestion of a necessary "subjective confirmation" growing out of a sacramentally "objective confirmation,"
the latter, however, being left undefined.[67]

Why Lutheran and Episcopalian Charismatics have
been so slow to articulate a theology of "Confirmation"
in terms of prayer for a baptism in the Holy Spirit
with a consequent manifestation of charismata is probably explainable psychologically as a "need for space"
- a space in which to develop an understanding of the
full New Testament teaching on baptism and the charismata, in order first then to engage their respective
churches on the meaning of the traditional Rite of Confirmation and how it needs to be integrated with their
own New Testament insights and "confirming" experience.
This book is an attempt to encourage just such serious
reflection on an issue which has not yet been sufficiently and ecumenically resolved in the Church

We cannot at this time, therefore, actually speak
of a clear position taken by advocates of charismatic
renewal on the question of its relation to the traditional practice of confirmation in the Church. In the
following concluding theses, however, I should like to
make this attempt, doing so on the basis of what I have
learned from Holy Scripture, the broad tradition of the
Church, and my own experience through involvement in
the charismatic renewal. Again, I will at best be representing the possible position of only some of those
involved in charismatic renewal, but I offer these
thoughts as theses for discussion in the hope of finding both a growing consensus among charismatics and a
growing rapprochement between those involved in liturgical renewal, pedagogical renewal, and charismatic renewal.

IV   Discussion Theses Regarding Confirmation and
      the Charismata

1. The word "confirmation" may legitimately describe
    the following situations in the church:

    a) God's "confirmation" of our new birth and iden-
       tity through baptismal faith by a reaffirmation
       of his promises to us through his Word (and
       sacraments).

    b) Our own "confirmation" of our new birth and
       identity through baptismal faith by (increas-
       ingly mature) reaffirmations of that faith.

    c) God's "confirmation" of our new birth and iden-
       tity through baptismal faith by his own ful-
       filling of his baptismally based promises to
       us in our experience (specifically, the mani-
       festation of "charismata") as we respond to
       these promises in faith-full obedience and
       prayer.

2. These three different types of "confirmation"
    correspond roughly to the central concerns of
    liturgical renewal (1a), pedagogical renewal (1b),
    and charismatic renewal (1c).

3. "Charismata" can be spoken of in both a broad and
    a narrow sense. Spoken of broadly, they include
    any manifestation of God's Spirit in our lives;
    spoken of narrowly, they refer especially to such
    manifestations of God's Spirit in our lives which
    because of their more unusual character have great-
    er "sign" value. Both types have a "confirming"
    effect, both types are needed, and both types
    should be expected and sought.

4. The following ages might be suggested as the most
    normally appropriate for each of the different
    types of "confirmation":

    a) Type 1a is always appropriate and necessary but
       might receive a more significant ritual expres-
       sion in connection with first communion around
       age 10 (grade 5).

    b) Type 1b is always appropriate and necessary but
       it is also to be understood relative to the in-
       dividual's growing maturity. Age 15 (grade 10)
       might be a particularly appropriate time to ex-
       pect the individual young believer to personally
       and publicly reaffirm his or her commitment to
       Christ and Christ's people.

    c) Type 1c is always appropriate and necessary but
       it is also to be understood relative to the in-
       dividual's growing maturity. Very young child-
       ren ought to be experiencing the confirmation
       which occurs with manifestly answered prayer.
       Older children can and may experience the mani-
       festation of confirming charismata as they make
       their own personal and public commitment to
       Christ and Christ's people (see 4b above). All
       believers ought to be experiencing frequent con-
       firmations through the manifestation of charis-
       mata as they pursue the doing of their Lord's
       will (discipleship) in faith-full obedience and
       prayer.

5. The three types of "confirmation," though necessar-
    ily distinguished, ought not be essentially separa-
    ted and divided from one another, just as grace,
    faith, and prayerful obedience ought neither be
    confused with nor divided from one another.

6. The tradition of a single, unrepeatable, and almost
    necessary "Rite of Confirmation" ought to be drop-
    ped, since it obscures the value of baptism and
    diminishes a necessary appreciation for the repeat-
    able confirmations the Lord intends for his people.
    Sometimes it even drives them to the confusion of
    "rebaptism" as a supposed remedy. Instead:

    a) Type 1a is best left without any special ritual
       (outside of, perhaps, first communion), taking
       place regularly simply by the faithful use of
       Word and sacraments.

b) Type 1b might be somewhat ritualized to draw
   special attention to its public, confessional
   character, but for all of that it should not
   be formalized to the point of depersonalization.
   This initial ritualized act will have to be followed by regular, sometimes planned and sometimes spontaneous, expressions of Christian confession and commitment. It would be better to
   call it a "personal confession of faith" rather
   than "Confirmation."

c) Type 1c will also follow a developmental pattern
   with frequent "confirmations" thus occurring.
   However, there is no reason why such a confirmation could not be prepared for and expected
   also in a more public context in connection with
   6b.

7. The laying on of hands may be an appropriate faith-
   stimulating gesture in connection with all three
   types:

   a) As a gesture of personal forgiveness and iden-
      tification with the community of the faithful.

   b) As a gesture of recognition and blessing after
      one's public commitment to Christ and Christ's
      people.

   c) As a gesture of personal prayer signalling an
      openness to receive any of God's confirming
      charismata.

8. The anointing with oil would appear to be most
   appropriate in connection with baptism. It might
   also be used elsewhere as a symbol of the Holy
   Spirit's work, but giving it express sacramental
   significance anywhere should be scrupulously avoid-
   ed, since there seems to be some connection between
   such liturgical usage and the diminished expectation of the Holy Spirit's experiential manifestation in the confirming charismata. Its use in connection with healing dare only be faith-stimulating,
   not sacramental. Healing is a gift of the Spirit;
   it is not the consequence of the anointing with oil
   as such. The latter can only be a symbol of what
   is expectantly awaited as an answer to faith-full
   obedience and prayer. When healing occurs, it
   serves as the confirming charism, not the oil.

9. Parish renewal is closely linked with a "holistic"
    view of "confirmation." Where the three types,
    currently represented by liturgical renewal, peda-
    gogical renewal, and charismatic renewal, are not
    properly integrated in parish life and ministry,
    renewal will be hampered, since Word and sacra-
    ments, faith (in its developmental fullness), and
    prayerful obedience dare not be separated from one
    another. Where they are, renewal will be thwarted.

Footnotes

[1]For example, Walter J. Hollenweger, The Pentecostals: The Charismatic Movement in the Churches (Minneapolis: Augsburg, 1972), pp.21-28.

[2]See above, pp.53-55; also the modern form of this
argument in Douglas Judisch, An Evaluation of Claims
to the Charismatic Gifts (Grand Rapids: Baker, 1978),
esp. pp.17-26.

[3]Hollenweger, op. cit., p. XVIII; Vinson Synan,
The Holiness-Pentecostal Movement in the United States
(Grand Rapids: Eerdmans, 1971), pp.185; 205-207.

[4]Even Dr. Henry Pitt Van Dusen, President emeritus
of Union Theological Seminary, New York, once suggested
that "the apostles might have found themselves more at
home in a Pentecostal or holiness assembly than in a
more traditional Christian worship service." Cf. Frederick Dale Bruner, A Theology of the Holy Spirit (Grand
Rapids: Eerdmans, 1970), pp.29-30.

[5]Hollenweger, op. cit., pp.3-20; Erling Jorstad,
The Holy Spirit in Today's Church: A Handbook of the
New Pentecostalism (Nashville: Abingdon, 1973), pp. 5;
16-28; 135-145.

[6]From the abundance of literature in this field I
cite only the following as particularly helpful: Ernest
B. Koenker, The Liturgical Renaissance in the Roman
Catholic Church, Second Edition (St. Louis: Concordia,
1966): Dale Moody, Baptism: Foundation for Christian
Unity (Philadelphia: Westminster, 1967); Aidan Kavanagh, The Shape of Baptism: The Rite of Christian Initiation (New York: Pueblo, 1978).

[7]Kavanagh, op. cit., p. 85. Here it is also contended that "charismatics" were capitalizing on the situation by their "gnostic and elitist" suggestion that confirmation be understood as what they had come to call "baptism in the Holy Spirit." Kavanagh cites none of the literature coming out of the "charismatic renewal." See, however, Stephen B. Clark, _Confirmation and the "Baptism of the Holy Spirit"_ (Pecos: Dove, 1969), esp. pp.9-15, where Clark argues for a "renewing of confirmation" through an experiential "baptism of the Holy Spirit" released through faith and prayer.

[8]Kavanagh, op. cit., pp.165; 180; 199.

[9]Ibid., pp.106; 109-122; 23-31; 177-180.

[10]Ibid., pp.106; 109-122; 23-31; 177-180.

[11]Neville Clark as quoted by Dale Moody, op. cit., p.271. It is said that a sacramental "service of blessing" might be more appropriate than baptism for infants. Ibid., p.250.

[12]Kavanagh, op. cit., pp.89-91; 195.

[13]Ibid., pp.85; 119f.; 167; 170; 182; 200.

[14]Ibid., pp.130; 168; 174.

[15]Cf. pp.47-48, 70 above.

[16]_The Rites of the Catholic Church as Revised by Decree of the Second Vatican Ecumenical Council and Published by Authority of Pope Paul VI_ (New York: Pueblo, 1976), p.290.

[17]Ibid., p.289.

[18]Ibid., pp.293-296; 116; 301; 310; 319; 325.

[19]Kavanagh, op. cit., pp.163-165.

[20]Ibid., pp.175; 196. Also Günter Biemer, "Controversy on the Age of Confirmation as a Typical Example of Conflict between the Criteria of Theology and the Demands of Pastoral Practice," in _Concilium 112 (2/1978): Liturgy and Human Passage,_ edited by David Power and Luis Maldonado (New York: Seabury, 1979), pp.115-125.

[21]Kavanagh, op. cit., p.183.

[22]See text to footnote 17 above; also _Rites_, pp.291-292.

[23]Kavanagh, op. cit., p.183.

[24]Koenker, op. cit., pp.VI-VII.

[25]Moody, pp.162-216.

[26]Ibid., p.214; Kavanagh, op. cit., pp.89-91; 175-176.

[27]Eugene L. Brand, _Baptism: A Pastoral Perspective_ (Minneapolis: Augsburg, 1975), pp.74-77; 86; 89; 93.

[28]Ibid., pp.24-25; 38-44; 79-86; 91-94; 98. Brand's concern, however, was not unambiguously upheld in the actual revised rites as proposed in the new _Lutheran Book of Worship_ (Minneapolis: Augsburg, 1978), pp.123-124, where the creedal questions are addressed to "the baptismal group and the congregation," although the baptismal formula itself as well as the consignation are clearly addressed to the baptismal candidate regardless of age.

[29]Ibid., pp.40-44; 92.

[30]_Lutheran Book of Worship_, pp.5; 198-201. Although the "Rite of Confirmation" in _Lutheran Worship_ (St. Louis: Concordia Publishing House, 1982), pp.205-207, appears more "traditional" and retains certain confessionalistic elements dropped in _Lutheran Book of Worship_, it too understands confirmation essentially as the confirmand's public affirmation of his or her baptism. Whereas the prayer for the Holy Spirit in LBW asks God the Father to "confirm his/her faith," LW omits this notion. Nevertheless, it is a liturgical scholar of the Lutheran Church Missouri Synod, Hans Boehringer, who has been most open to understanding confirmation as God's work through the manifestation of the Spirit's gifts. See his "Baptism, Confirmation and First Communion: Christian Initiation in the Contemporary Church" in _Institute of Liturgical Studies Occasional Papers, Number 1, Christian Initiation: Reborn of Water and the Spirit_, ed. D. Brockopp, B. Helge, D. Truemper (Valparaiso: Institute of Liturgical Studies, 1981), pp.84-87.

[31]Brand, op. cit., p.113.

[32]Ibid., pp.107-108.

[33]Ibid., pp.38; 112-113; 122.

[34]Ibid., pp.22; 58; 76-77; 109.

[35]Ibid., pp.35; 38; 40; 92; 121.

[36]Thomas A. Droege, Self-Realization and Faith: Beginning and Becoming in Relation to God (Chicago: Lutheran Education Association, 1978), esp. the chapters entitled "Faith and Human Development," pp.35-48, and "Baptism and Trust," pp.51-69; see also Robert Conrad, "Books Worth Discussing: James W. Fowler, Stages of Faith: The Psychology of Human Development and the Quest for Meaning" in Currents in Theology and Mission, Vol. 9, No. 3 (June, 1982), pp.178-180; and Thomas A. Droege, "The Formation of Faith in Christian Initiation: A Disputation" in The Cresset, Vol XLVI, No. 6 (April, 1983), pp.16-23.

[37]Ibid., pp.47-48.

[38]Biemer, op. cit., pp.116-117.

[39]Kent S. Knutson, "A Theological Perspective," in Confirmation and Education, ed. by W. Kent Gilbert (Philadelphia: Fortress, 1969), pp.53-54.

[40]Aidan Kavanagh, "Life-Cycle Events, Civil Ritual and the Christian," in Concilium 112 (2/1978): Liturgy and Human Passage, edited by David Power and Luis Maldonado (New York: Seabury, 1979), p.17; Droege, op. cit., pp.81;83.

[41]Droege, op. cit., p.52

[42]Ibid., p.77.

[43]Ibid., p.42.

[44]These four complementary descriptions of faith can all be found frequently and in close proximity in Melanchthon's "Apology of the Augsburg Confession," Article IV on "Justification." See The Book of Concord, ed. by Tappert, pp.113-117, ¶¶ 48-74. Also Theodore Jungkuntz, A Lutheran Charismatic Catechism (Flushing, N.Y.: Bread of Life Ministries, 1979), pp.8-10.

[45]Droege, op. cit., pp.57-59.

⁴⁶Kavanagh, <u>Concilium 112</u> (fn. 40 above), pp.16-17; 22-23.

⁴⁷Ibid., p.23.

⁴⁸Droege, op. cit., pp.88-90. For a critique of Droege's neglect of the theme of baptismal death and daily repentance in his developmental model, see the review of his book by Paul Pfotenhauer in <u>The Cresset</u>, Vol. XLI, No. 8 (June, 1978), p.27.

⁴⁹George T. Montague, <u>The Holy Spirit: Growth of a Biblical Tradition</u> (New York: Paulist, 1976), pp.333-365.

⁵¹<u>Luther's Works, American Edition</u>, Vol. 41, "Church and Ministry III" (Philadelphia: Fortress, 1966), pp.113-115.

⁵² Karlfried Froelich, "Charismatic Manifestations and the Lutheran Incarnational Stance," in <u>The Holy Spirit in the Life of the Church</u>, ed. by Paul D. Opsahl (Minneapolis: Augsburg, 1978), pp.150-155; cf. also Bengt R. Hoffman, <u>Luther and the Mystics</u> (Minneapolis: Augsburg, 1976), pp.101-102; 185; 195; 226; 229-231.

⁵³George H. Williams and Edith Waldvogel, "A History of Speaking in Tongues and Related Gifts," in <u>The Charimatic Movement</u>, ed. by Michael P. Hamilton (Grand Rapids: Eerdmans, 1975), pp.70-75. Also see above, pp.53-55; 58.

⁵⁴Richard A. Jensen, <u>Touched By the Spirit</u> (Minneapolis: Augsburg, 1975), pp.36-38.

⁵⁵Froelich, op. cit., p.151. Cf. WA 10:3, 145f.

⁵⁶Dietrich Bonhoeffer, <u>The Cost of Discipleship</u> (New York: Macmillan, 1959), pp.35-47; 79. For Luther on the Gospel's "cost" see his Large Catechism on "Confession" (Tappert, op. cit., LC VI, 6 - p.457).

⁵⁷See above, pp.45-46.

⁵⁸Roland Bainton, <u>Here I Stand: A Life of Martin Luther</u> (New York: Abingdon-Cokesbury, 1950), p.65.

⁵⁹Very helpful to me has been the vivid analogy used by Fr. Kilian McDonnell of a line from A to Z representing the full spectrum of how the Spirit comes to visibility in a variety of charisms and how our exper-

ience of those charisms tends to increase as we allow
our expectancy to be increased by including not only
those charisms represented by A to P but also those
from P to Z. Cf. <u>Theological and Pastoral Orientations
on the Catholic Charismatic Renewal. Malines Document 1</u>
(Ann Arbor: Servant Books, 1974), p.17.

[60]Jungkuntz, <u>A Lutheran Charismatic Catechism</u>, pp.
5-6.

[61]Ibid., pp.6-8.

[62]See above, pp.86-88.

[63]Koenig, op. cit., pp.163-164; 174-177. Here the
author reviews positions taken within charismatic renewal as to how the manifestation of charismata cata-
lyzes the growth of eschatological community.

[64]Stephen B. Clark, <u>Confirmation and the "Baptism
of the Holy Spirit"</u> (Pecos: Dove, 1969); Donald L. Gelpi,
<u>Pentecostalism: A Theological Viewpoint</u> (New York:
Paulist, 1971), pp.181-184; Charles Antekeier, Van and
Janet Vandagriff, <u>Confirmation: The Power of the Spirit.
A Charismatic Preparation Program for Youth, their par-
ents and Sponsors</u> (Notre Dame: Ave Maria, 1972); Judith
Tydings, <u>Gathering a People</u> (Plainfield: Logos, 1977),
pp.251-268; Heribert Mühlen, <u>A Charismatic Theology:
Initiation in the Spirit</u> (New York: Paulist, 1978),
p.351; Tim Lenton, "Renewal in the New Hebrides," in
<u>Acts 29. Newsletter of the Episcopal Renewal Ministries</u>,
May, 1981, p.3.

[65]This tension is found between liturgical renewal
and pedagogical renewal even independently of its com-
plication by the addition of charismatic renewal. Note
the difference between Kavanagh, Biemer, and Droege
cited above, pp.86-87.

[66]Antekeier, Vandagriff, op. cit., pp.15-23, esp.
p.19. This notion has been severely criticized by
Aidan Kavanagh, <u>The Shape of Baptism</u>, p.85.

[67]Tydings, op. cit., p.264.

BIBLIOGRAPHY

Antekeier, Charles, and Vandagriff, Van and Janet.
Confirmation: The Power of the Spirit. A Charismatic
Preparation Program for Youth, their Parents and Spon-
sors. Notre Dame: Ave Maria, 1972.

Bainton, Roland H. Erasmus of Christendom. London:
Collins, 1970.

__________. Here I Stand: A Life of Martin
Luther. New York: Abingdon-Cokesbury, 1950.

Biemer, Günter. "Controversy on the Age of Confirmation
as a Typical Example of Conflict between the Criteria of
Theology and the Demands of Pastoral Practice" in Liturgy and Human Passage, ed. David Power and Luis Maldonado, Concilium Series 112, 115-125. New York: Seabury,
1979.

Boehringer, Hans. "Baptism, Confirmation and First Communion: Christian Initiation in the Contemporary Church"
in Institute of Liturgical Studies Occasional Papers,
Number 1, Christian Initiation: Reborn of Water and the
Spirit, ed. D. Brockopp, B. Helge, D. Truemper. Pp.73-
98. Valparaiso, Indiana: Institute of Liturgical Studies, 1981.

Bohen, Marian. The Mystery of Confirmation: A Theology
of the Sacrament. New York: Herder, 1963.

Bonhoeffer, Dietrich. The Cost of Discipleship. New
York: Macmillan, 1959.

Brand, Eugene L. Baptism: A Pastoral Perspective.
Minneapolis: Augsburg, 1975.

Bromiley, Geoffrey W. "Thomas Cranmer" in Reformers in
Profile, 165-191. B. A. Gerrish, ed. Philadelphia:
Fortress, 1967.

Brown, Dale. Understanding Pietism. Grand Rapids:
Eerdmans, 1978.

Bruner, Frederick Dale. A Theology of the Holy Spirit.
Grand Rapids: Eerdmans, 1970

Burgess, Joseph A., and Igleheart, Glenn A. "Lutheran-
Baptist Dialogue" in American Baptist Quarterly, Vol.1
No. 2 (Dec., 1982), pp.99-215.

Calvin, John. _Institutes of the Christian Religion,
Vol. II._ Henry Beveridge, trans. Grand Rapids: Eerdmans, 1957.

_Canons and Decrees of the Council of Trent. Original
Texts with English Translation._ J.H. Schroeder, trans.
St. Louis: Herder, 1941.

Clark, Stephen B. _Confirmation and the "Baptism of the
Holy Spirit."_ Pecos: Dove, 1969.

Chemnitz, Martin. _Examination of the Council of Trent,
Part II._ Fred Kramer, trans. St. Louis: Concordia,
1978.

Cherry, Conrad. _The Theology of Jonathan Edwards: A
Reappraisal._ Garden City: Doubleday, 1966.

Conrad, Robert. "Books Worth Discussing: James W. Fowler. Stages of Faith: The Psychology of Human Development and the Quest for Meaning" in _Currents in Theology
and Mission_, Vol. 9, No. 3 (June 1982), pp.178-180.

Cully, K. B., ed. _Confirmation: History, Doctrine and
Practice._ Greenwich: Seabury, 1962.

Dix, Gregory. _The Theology of Confirmation in relation
to Baptism._ Westminster: Dacre, 1946.

Dolan, John P. _History of the Reformation: A Conciliatory Assessment of Opposite Views._ New York: Desalee,
1965.

Droege, Thomas A. _Self-Realization and Faith: Beginning and Becoming in Relation to God._ Chicago: Lutheran Education Assoc., 1978.

__________________. "The Formation of Faith in Christian Initiation: A Disputation" in _The Cresset_, Vol.
XLVI, No. 6 (April, 1983), pp.16-23.

Dunn, James D. G. _Baptism in the Holy Spirit: A Reexamination of the New Testament Teaching on the Gift
of the Spirit in relation to Pentecostalism today._
Philadelphia: The Westminster Press, 1970.

Du Plessis, David J. _The Spirit Bade Me Go. Revised
Edition._ Plainfield: Logos, 1970.

Fisher, J.D.C. _Christian Initiation. Baptism in the
Medieval West._ London: SPCK, 1965.

__________. _Christian Initiation. The Reformation Period_. London: SPCK, 1970.

Fransen, Piet. "Confirmation" in _Sacramentum Mundi: An Encyclopedia of Theology, Vol. 1_. New York: Herder, 1968.

Froelich, Karlfried. "Charismatic Manifestations and the Lutheran Incarnational Stance" in _The Holy Spirit in the Life of the Church_, 136-157. Paul D. Opsahl, ed. Minneapolis: Augsburg, 1978.

Frör, Kurt, ed. _Confirmatio: Forschungen zur Geschichte und Praxis der Konfirmation_. München: Evang. Presseverband für Bayern, 1959

Gelpi, Donald L. _Pentecostalism: A Theological Viewpoint_. New York: Paulist, 1978.

Gerrish, B. A. "John Calvin" in _Reformers in Profile_, 142-164. B. A. Gerrish, ed. Philadelphia: Fortress, 1967.

Grant, Robert. "Development of the Christian Catechumenate." In _Made, Not Born_, 32-49. Notre Dame: University of Notre Dame, 1976.

Hamilton, Michael P., ed. _The Charismatic Movement_. Grand Rapids: Eerdmans, 1975.

Hoffman, Bengt R. _Luther and the Mystics_. Minneapolis: Augsburg, 1976.

Hollenweger, Walter J. _The Pentecostals: The Charismatic Movement in the Churches_. Minneapolis: Augsburg, 1972.

Jenson, Richard A. _Touched By the Spirit_. Minneapolis: Augsburg, 1975.

Jewett, Paul K. _Infant Baptism and the Covenant of Grace_. Grand Rapids: Eerdmans, 1978.

Jordahn, Ottfried. _Georg Friedrich Seilers Beitrag zur Praktischen Theologie der kirchlichen Aufklärung_. Nürnberg: Selbstverlag des Vereins für bayerische Kirchengeschichte, 1970.

Jorstad, Erling. _The Holy Spirit in Today's Church: A Handbook of the New Pentecostalism_. Nashville: Abingdon, 1973.

Judisch, Douglas. _An Evaluation of Claims to the Charismatic Gifts_. Grand Rapids: Baker, 1978.

Jungkuntz, Richard. _The Gospel of Baptism_. St. Louis:
Concordia, 1968.

Jungkuntz, Theodore. _A Lutheran Charismatic Catechism_.
Flushing, N.Y.: Bread of Life Ministries, 1979.

Kavanagh, Aidan. "Life-Cycle Events, Civil Ritual and
the Christian" in _Liturgy and Human Passage_, ed. David
Power and Luis Maldonado, Concilium Series 112, 14-24.
New York: Seabury, 1979.

__________. _The Shape of Baptism: The Rite of
Christian Initiation_. New York: Pueblo, 1978.

Kierkegaard, Sören. _Attack upon "Christendom_." Walter
Lowrie, trans. Boston: Beacon, 1944

Klos, Frank W. _Confirmation and First Communion_.
Minneapolis: Augsburg, 1968.

Knutson, Kent S. "A Theological Perspective," in _Con-
firmation and Education_, 53-64. W. Kent Gilbert, ed.
Philadelphia: Fortress, 1969.

Koenig, John. _Charismata: God's Gifts for God's Peo-
ple_. Philadelphia: Westminster, 1978.

Koenker, Ernest B. _The Liturgical Renaissance in the
Roman Catholic Church_, Second Edition. St. Louis:
Concordia, 1966.

Kucharek, Casimir. _The Sacramental Mysteries: A Byzantine Approach_. Allendale: Alleluia, 1976.

Lampe, G.W.H. _The Seal of the Spirit_. London: SPCK,
1951.

Lazareth, William H. and Nikos Nissiotis, eds. _Baptism,
Eucharist and Ministry_. Geneva: World Council of
Churches, 1982.

Lovelace, Richard F. _Dynamics of Spiritual Life: An
Evangelical Theology of Renewal_. Downers Grove: Inter-
Varsity, 1979.

Lutheran Book of Worship. Minneapolis: Augsburg, 1978.

Lutheran Worship. St. Louis: Concordia, 1982.

Luther's Works. American Edition. 55 Volumes. Jaroslav Pelikan and Helmut T. Lehmann, eds. St. Louis and Philadelphia: Concordia and Fortress.

Made, Not Born. New Perspectives on Christian Initiation and the Catechumenate, ed. Murphy Center for Liturgical Research. Notre Dame: University of Notre Dame, 1976.

Marty, Martin E. Righteous Empire: The Protestant Experience in America. New York: Dial, 1970.

Maurer, Wilhelm. "Geschichte von Firmung und Konfirmation bis zum Ausgang der lutherischen Orthodoxie" in Confirmatio, 9-38. Kurt Frör, ed. München: Evang. Presseverband für Bayern, 1959.

McDonnell, Kilian, ed. Theological and Pastoral Orientations on the Catholic Charismatic Renewal. Malines Document 1. Ann Arbor: Servant Books, 1974.

McNally, Robert E. "Ignatius Loyola" in Reformers in Profile, 232-256. B. A. Gerrish, ed. Philadelphia: Fortress, 1967.

Mitchell, Leonel L. Baptismal Anointing. London: SPCK, 1966.

Mitchell, Nathan D. "Dissolution of the Rite of Christian Initiation." In Made, Not Born, 50-82. Notre Dame: University of Notre Dame, 1976.

Montague, George T. The Holy Spirit: Growth of a Biblical Tradition. Paramus: Paulist, 1976.

Montgomery, John Warwick. Principalities and Powers. Minneapolis: Augsburg, 1976.

Moody, Dale. Baptism: Foundation for Christian Unity. Philadelphia: Westminster, 1967.

Mühlen, Heribert. A Charismatic Theology. Initiation in the Spirit. New York: Paulist, 1978.

Nigg, Walter. Warriors of God: The Great Religious Orders and their Founders. Mary Ilford, trans. London: Secker and Warburg, 1959.

O'Conner, Edward D. Perspectives on Charismatic Renewal. Notre Dame: University of Notre Dame, 1975.

Prenter, Regin. _Spiritus Creator_. Philadelphia: Muhlenberg/Fortress, 1953.

Reed, Luther D. _The Lutheran Liturgy_. Philadelphia: Fortress, 1947.

Repp, Arthur C. _Confirmation in the Lutheran Church_. St. Louis: Concordia, 1964.

Rilliet, Jean. _Zwingli: Third Man of the Reformation_. Harold Knight, trans. Philadelphia: Westminster, 1959/64.

Schleiermacher, Friedrich. _The Christian Faith, Vol.2_. H. R. Mackintosh and J. S. Stewart, eds. New York: Harper and Row, 1963.

Spittler, Russell P., ed. _Perspectives on the New Pentecostalism_. Grand Rapids: Baker, 1976.

Stagg, Frank, with Hinson, E. Glenn, and Oates, Wayne E. _Glossolalia: Tongue Speaking in Biblical, Historical, and Psychological Perspective_. Nashville: Abingdon, 1967.

Stenzel, Alois. "Temporal and Supra-Temporal in the History of the Catechumenate and Baptism: in _Adult Baptism and the Catechumenate_, ed. Johannes Wagner, Concilium Series 22, 31-44. New York: Paulist, 1967.

Stevich, Daniel B. "Christian Initiation: Post Reformation to the Present Era." In _Made, Not Born_, Notre Dame: University of Notre Dame, 1976.

Stupperich, Robert. _Melanchthon_. Robert H. Fischer, trans. Philadelphia: Westminster, 1955.

Synan, Vinson. _The Holiness-Pentecostal Movement in the United States_. Grand Rapids: Eerdmans, 1971.

The Book of Concord: The Confessions of the Evangelical Lutheran Church. Theodore G. Tappert, ed. Philadelphia: Fortress, 1959.

The Loci Communes of Philip Melanchthon. Charles L. Hill, trans. Boston: Meador, 1944.

The Rites of the Catholic Church as Revised by Decree of the Second Vatican Ecumenical Council and Published by Authority of Pope Paul VI. New York: Pueblo, 1976.

Thielicke, Helmut, <u>I Believe: The Christian's Creed</u>.
Philadelphia: Fortress, 1968.

Thompson, Bard. "Ulrich Zwingli" in <u>Reformers in Pro-
file</u>, 115-141. B. A. Gerrish, ed. Philadelphia: Fortress, 1967.

Tydings, Judith. <u>Gathering A People: Catholic Saints
in Charismatic Perspective</u>. Plainfield: Logos, 1977.

Van de Poll, G. J. <u>Martin Bucer's Liturgical Ideas</u>.

Whitaker, E. C. <u>Documents of the Baptismal Liturgy</u>.
London: SPCK, 1960.

ABOUT THE AUTHOR

Theodore R. Jungkuntz received his B.A. from North-
western College in Watertown, Wisconsin, in 1953; his
M.A. in classical languages and archeology from the
University of Missouri in 1954; his B.D. from Wisconsin
Lutheran Seminary in Mequon, Wisconsin, in 1958; and
his Dr. Theol. from Friedrich Alexander University in
Erlangen, Germany, in 1962. He was ordained and received into the ministerium of the Lutheran Church
Missouri Synod in 1963. After a short period in the
pastoral ministry he began his teaching career as Assist-
ant Professor of Classical Languages at Saint Paul's
College in Concordia, Missouri, from 1964-1966, and
since 1966 he has taught theology at Valparaiso University in Valparaiso, Indiana, where he now holds the
rank of Professor of Theology.

His doctoral dissertation led him into a study of
the Lutheran Church Orders of the sixteenth century.
It was in this connection that he developed a special
interest in the theology and practice of confirmation.
In 1968 he became involved in Lutheran Charismatic
Renewal and since then he has published many articles
relating charismatic experience to Lutheran confessional theology. He has also published a book on church
unity entitled <u>Formulators of the Formula of Concord:
Four Architects of Lutheran Unity</u> (St. Louis: Concordia Publishing House, 1977).